W9-CKJ-053

Also by Kent Durden

GIFTS OF AN EAGLE
FLIGHT TO FREEDOM

A
FINE AND

PEACEFUL KINGDOM

Kent Durden

Simon and Schuster   New York

Copyright © 1975 by Kent Durden
All rights reserved
including the right of reproduction
in whole or in part in any form
Published by Simon and Schuster
Rockefeller Center, 630 Fifth Avenue
New York, New York 10020

Designed by Elizabeth Woll
Manufactured in the United States of America

1   2   3   4   5   6   7   8   9   10

Library of Congress Cataloging in Publication Data

Durden, Kent.
  A fine and peaceful kingdom.

    1. Animals, Legends and stories of. I. Title.
QL791.D857   591   74-26967
ISBN 0-671-21959-6

to Kim and Kris

CONTENTS

FOREWORD

For many people, it isn't until long after they have been established in the everyday drudgery of making a living and meeting responsibilities that they realize that their personal interests are far distant from the reality of what they are actually doing. This can be a sad awakening, or it can be a turning point—a revitalizing quest for more rewarding involvements, for a new sense of values or even for a new life style to equalize the balance once again.

In my case, I was fortunate in recognizing early in life that my main interest, the thing I loved best, was to learn about nature and animals and life outdoors. Raised as I was in a rural setting in the mountains of California, and influenced by my father, who was ever encouraging about enjoying and observing the animals around us, appreciation of my environment became an intrinsic part of my life. As I grew up, it became apparent to me that it would have to be a part of my life work. When the time came to make a choice about what that work would be, I chose wildlife cinematography. It seemed the perfect involvement, a way of satisfying my own desire to learn more about animals and at the same time passing it along to others through my work. I have never once regretted that choice.

I am the first to admit that by scientific standards my work is somewhat inconsequential. I can add nothing to the excellent work of scientists—the population studies, genetic explorations, vital statistics and countless other contributions to our knowledge of species. Theirs is a specialized area of study that is crucial to the survival of animals in this world. But no less important is my own specialty—the study of the personal side of animals, as individuals in their natural habitats. I think that what I have seen with the amateur's eye can indeed help the average person to appreciate animals and can help bridge the gap between us humans and what we call the "lower animals."

In dealing with animals, especially in the field of movie making, it is easy to be accused of exploiting them for commercial purposes. I feel that there are definitely too many examples of this, at the animals' expense. However, it would be unwise and unfair to assume that all animal or nature photographers fall into this category.

Whether filming wild animals or tamed ones, it is important to maintain respect and consideration for the subjects. The conscientious photographer assumes the responsibility for the animal's well-being. There is a delicate fringe area upon which man can intrude in a creature's life without disturbing it harmfully. When filming wildlife, it is imperative to understand and respect these boundaries.

In filming animals under controlled situations it is important that an animal not be portrayed as doing something that it would not normally do. It has never been my purpose to make circus actors out of my subjects. I believe in allowing them to behave as normally as possible. Making a nature film with a story line requires a certain amount of manipulation or control, but at all times the animal should feel that it has control even though it doesn't. If the animal is at all forced to behave in a certain way, it will inevitably become defensive and nervous. And with all candid behavior lost, so is the purpose of the film. There are times when control may slip away from the photographer to the animal, resulting in disastrous but often comical scenes.

More important to me than the scenes I have captured on film are the actual experiences themselves. As a result of my work, I now feel that I "know" personally countless individuals in the animal world. I feel I know them as well as I know human friends. It's impossible to know friends without being concerned for them. Consequently, I find myself concerned for all wildlife. It is my hope that others will gain this same concern and that we, as the dominant species of the animal world, will assume the responsibility that is ours for the preservation of our wildlife citizens.

KENT DURDEN

1
FIRST EXPOSURES

The twin beams of the headlights pierced the blackness, illuminating the country road ahead of the automobile. With face pressed against the side window, a small boy peered out at the night. As an eight-year-old, I always relished those six-mile drives home at night after visits to town. There were few lights along the way, but there were many things to be seen, and through a youngster's eyes even the most ordinary became exciting.

Pieces of glass or bottles heaved by motorists off into the brush became, in the lights of the car, the flashing eyes of lions or wolves lurking in the darkness, just waiting for unwary cars to stop. Frequently the ghostly shape of a barn owl would fly across the road, its white wings flashing weirdly as it disappeared into the darkness. Occasionally, jackrabbits, with huge ears erect, would bound across the road and into the brush, to be eaten, no doubt, by the lions and wolves. There were those times, too, when we spotted real bobcats or coyotes caught briefly in the car lights. But for some reason the real animals were always a bit of a disappointment when compared to the "big ones" whose eyes reflected in the darkness and whose bodies existed entirely in my imagination.

Our car turned off the paved country road and began the last half mile up a dirt road to our house. We hadn't gone more than a hundred yards when Dad stopped the car and pointed to something ahead. It was very small and black and looked quite harmless. Dad was always one to investigate. I elected to remain in the car, however, and let him brave the unknown. Soon he returned with something cupped in his hands. By his grin we all knew that we were about to gain another addition to the family.

"A baby skunk," he announced happily, and climbed in. It was a striped skunk that had for some reason been separated from its mother. We hurried on home to warm some milk for our new family member.

Being situated far back in a forest of eucalyptus trees, our home was ideally suited for enjoying nature. It was in central coastal California several miles from the ocean, on a forested plateau that the local people called "the mesa." The eucalyptus were the most common trees I knew for the first ten years of my life. Although these tall trees provided a dense forest, a quick glance would reveal to anyone that it was not a natural forest. The trees were laid out in a regular pattern, row upon row of trees covering thousands of acres of the mesa top. Forty years before, an enterprising man had imported them from Australia and planted the entire mesa top in what he thought would be a hugely profitable business venture to corner the market on a fabulous wood for furniture making. It was an ill-planned move, since eucalyptus wood cannot be cured without splitting. Nevertheless, his efforts now were clearly visible in the neatly laid-out forest that covered over ten square miles. Not entirely worthless, the wood makes excellent firewood, and sections were thinned regularly for that purpose.

Just as pine forests are noted for their special scent, the eucalyptus forest has its own aroma. Eucalyptus leaves contain a volatile resin which smells like Vick's Vaporub. In fact, old-timers claim that the vapor from boiled eucalyptus will clear up a cold in no time. When the dense, moist fog rolled in from the sea and filtered through the trees, bathing each leaf, the aroma became very strong. Strangely enough, I loved this smell and breathed deeply on those damp mornings. It was a bit like living in a giant Vick's Vaporizer.

Wildlife was abundant in the forest, and there were many nocturnal visitors to our place. There were always a few tamed animals or birds of some kind in our household. Often they were injured or orphaned creatures brought to us by people. My earliest recollections of pets were these animals that became a part of the family for a time and enriched our lives with their interesting habits. This was just the beginning of a long history of animals and birds in my life. At the time we found the skunk, we also had a Cooper's hawk, a gray fox and a very ordinary house cat.

Since the skunk came to us fully armed, it was inevitable that we would experience his chemical-warfare capabilities sooner or later. As it worked out, it was sooner rather than later. A couple of days after his adoption we went into town. Before leaving, Dad placed him in a large pasteboard box. Just to be certain he wouldn't get loose, Dad put the box inside a large walk-in cage. The fact that the large cage also housed our Cooper's hawk didn't worry us. The hawk too was a youngster, barely able to hop about, and was confined to a far corner of the cage. There was no possibility, we thought, for the two to meet.

Later that afternoon as we turned off the paved road toward home, we detected the unmistakable odor of skunk. But, since we were still half a mile from home, Dad dismissed our inevitable suspicions. "He's much too small to create a stink that we could smell from so far away," he assured us. But as we drew closer the odor became stronger, and when we pulled up in front of the house there was no question in anyone's mind that we had arrived at the source of the stink. We raced to the cage and stood there gasping for breath and staring with disbelief at the sight.

The hawk, for some unexplained reason, had decided to try her wings. Apparently she had tried to hop up to her perch, had missed her mark, and had landed squarely inside the box with the skunk. From there on it was quite obvious. In one corner was the tiny skunk, business end pointed toward the other corner, where cowered the hawk, face and eyes covered with yellow, odoriferous fluid. The hawk was immobilized and practically blinded. The situation might have been comical had it not been for the misery the poor hawk was enduring. Dad quickly gathered her up and washed her thoroughly beneath a water tap. After several washings with soda and water, the bedraggled and shaken hawk was replaced in her cage, minus the skunk. She recovered in a few hours, but it was several days before the premises returned to normal.

The skunk, whom we named Stamper for his habit of stamping

his front feet when he was annoyed, never again used his powers of chemical warfare as long as we had him. He became a part of the family and entertained us for hours at a time. Our gray fox was a constant pest to Stamper. We constantly expected Stamper to teach the fox a lesson, but he always held his fire. Whenever the fox showed up, Stamper immediately stamped his tiny forefeet as a warning and then whirled to show the fox his business end. If the fox persisted in annoying him, Stamper would arch his tail so far over his head that it appeared to pull his whole rear section off the ground. Standing on only his front feet, he demonstrated an uncanny ability to maneuver so as to keep his tail section aimed at the fox. The fox, in turn, possessed an incredible knack of annoying Stamper to the very brink of disaster before abruptly breaking off the encounter.

When Stamper grew larger, he took up residence in an abandoned toolshed some distance from the house. His home was under the floor, with access through a missing board. For several months he lived there, sleeping by day and roaming by night. Once a day we would put a bowl of milk next to the hole and knock on the floor. In a moment a black nose would quiver at the entrance, to be followed by a pair of beady eyes, and Stamper would emerge to drink the milk and have his head scratched. After several months he disappeared. Wandered off, no doubt, to some other part of the forest.

Stamper's chief annoyance, the fox, stayed around considerably longer. He was much more a pet and had been with us from the time he was a kit. He was about a third grown when the manager of a nearby duck-hunting club brought him to us in a box after having accidentally caught him in a steel trap. His right paw was badly broken and he was weak and frightened from his ordeal. His soft gray fur was matted and dirty. He huddled in the box, trembling, and staring at us with dark-brown eyes filled with fear. Dad took the pitiful creature to the kitchen table and began first aid. I looked on with great interest and compassion as he tenderly splintered the small leg and bound it tightly with adhesive tape. Afterward we managed to force-feed the kit a small bit of meat, and then he was placed in a darkened box.

Next morning, alert and wild-eyed, he snapped his tiny jaws at our extended hands. An offering of food was sniffed but not eaten until we left the room. Within three days, however, the little fellow wandered awkwardly about the room, peering at us from beneath chairs and from behind bookcases. A week later he was frolicking without fear in the living room, playing with objects that we tossed for him. The family cat became his best friend. Upon seeing the cat, the fox would utter squeals of delight and throw himself at his friend, and the two would spend hours tussling and frolicking on the floor.

Once he was accustomed to the house, we decided to allow him outside. I have never enjoyed seeing animals in cages, and if one lives in a remote place it is quite a joy to have animal pets living free on the premises. There was no danger of his leaving, at least not while he was young.

Soon Foxy acquainted himself with every part of the area. He was still handicapped somewhat by the splint, but it didn't slow him down too much. He and the cat immediately took up their games outdoors, with greater gusto than before—as we found out that night after we had gone to bed.

Our place had a large wooden porch with steps at each end. Periodically throughout the night, the fox and the cat would race across the porch at high speed. In the first lap across the porch the cat was ahead and the rhythmic sound made by its padded feet wasn't too disturbing. But with the fox it was different. As he landed on the porch his feet produced three soft pads, followed by a loud clunk when his splinted foot hit the wooden boards. Three pads and a clunk, three pads and a clunk, across the porch and down the steps. Then the night became quiet again as their chase carried them off into the woods. As might be expected, just when we were almost asleep they came around for the second lap. This time the fox was in the lead. Three pads and a clunk, followed by the cat's soft padded footsteps. After one night of this activity something had to be done. A simple blockade at each of the outside stairs stopped the nocturnal Grand Prix across the porch.

In four weeks' time the splint was removed and our little gray fox was whole again. Now he could dig holes and even practice the gray foxes' unique trait of tree climbing. He soon found an old fir tree that leaned at quite an angle. Up in the crotch of the tree was an abandoned wood rat's nest. Foxy soon remodeled the pile of sticks until he had a nice, airy roost. Of all the members of the dog family, the gray fox is the only one that regularly practices tree climbing. In fact, in some areas he is called the tree fox. Our fox spent many happy hours snoozing up there in the nest or just lying with his head over the edge, watching the activities below. Although this refuge wasn't exactly catproof, it did provide an excellent rest from his raids on Stamper the skunk. It also provided a refuge for an eight-year-old boy. Often I would climb the tree and lie down beside Foxy, and we would spend hours there together.

Our Cooper's hawk rapidly gained her wings. Her first flights were awkward, wobbly affairs, usually from one fence post to another. The Cooper's hawk is a fast, maneuverable predator adapted especially well for short dashes through woods in pursuit of birds. In watching the first flights, one could hardly believe that she would ever amount to anything. But experience was the flight instructor, and soon the hawk was sitting atop the house.

We decided to let her fly at hack (free) around the property. Young hawks will often stay about the homestead for months, just as they do in the wild. Food was tossed to her each day, but no attempt was made to train her. After a day and a half on the roof, she decided to conquer new heights. No one to make hasty decisions, the hawk eyed first one target and then the other as the next likely landing spot. Finally, with a flourish of wings, off she went, gaining speed downhill, and then swooping up to land in, of all places, Foxy's nest. Needless to say, the fox was startled by this invasion of his privacy. He wasted no time bounding out of the tree and down to the house. From beneath the porch he peered up at his roost with its new tenant. This was the beginning of a feud between the hawk and the fox, one in which the fox was always the loser.

For the first couple of weeks the hawk was occupied with the task of perfecting her flying technique. Once she was sure of her new-found talent, her attention was drawn to play. Young hawks are quite playful and often use twigs, rocks, and other inanimate objects as their toys. So it was, one day, when the hawk was in a particularly playful mood. She had just "killed," without mercy, a dangerous clod of dirt and was perched on the housetop, her yellow eyes searching the ground below, when Foxy most inopportunely wandered down his tree and across the field toward the feeding pan on the porch. The hawk watched intently as Foxy made his way from bush to bush, and then, without warning, she dropped off the roof and plummeted toward him.

It wasn't the first time the fox had seen the hawk, of course, but it was the first time the hawk had come his way with such determination. Foxy immediately whirled and raced for his tree, with the hawk in hot pursuit. It must be pointed out that the gray fox is far too large an animal for the Cooper's hawk to capture; the hawk's only intention was play. Not being aware of this, the fox was doing his best to gain the safety of his tree nest. As he ran, his long bushy tail waved enticingly behind like a banner. It was this bushy tail that became the target of the hawk, an elusive target that was especially exciting because of its close proximity to the fox. The gap was closed quickly, but not before Foxy made it to his refuge. The hawk swooped up to land in a nearby tree.

From this time on the hawk watched constantly for Foxy. Any daylight stroll that Foxy took had to be planned with utmost care. He never knew exactly where the hawk was, so the less he exposed himself, the better. There were many times, however, when in spite of Foxy's precautions he would find the Cooper's hawk on his tail, literally. All she wanted to do was touch it—and touch it she did. The hawk finally became so expert at surprising Foxy that the last two inches of his beautiful tail became hairless, the result of countless grapplings of the hawk's talons.

Not all the creatures around our place were domesticated. There were many wild birds and animals that visited only at night. Among these were the great horned owls that began to appear about dusk. Their throaty hoots used to send a tingle down my spine as I lay in bed. Often, during early summer, young horned owls could be heard off in the forest trying their voices. Occasionally a young one would take a perch atop our chimney and begin its practice session. The mixture of squawks, raspy notes, and other indescribable sounds that emanated from the chimney top were so unreal that one would never guess they came from a horned owl. Once or twice a night a

Our first great horned owl, still in white down stage.

partial hoot would be heard as the owl triumphantly hit the right note. As summer progressed, the young owls' voices improved until they could make a tolerable imitation of their parents.

A favorite perching spot for the owls was on the gable of our barn some one hundred yards away. Often we would sit on the back porch during the late summer evenings and watch the owls arrive. Several times we saw one of them drop to the ground to catch a mouse or other small rodent. One evening an idea germinated in Dad's mind at this sight.

The next afternoon I followed Dad around as he prepared for the night's performance. First he set several traps in gopher holes which surrounded our house and garden. If there was one thing we had a surplus of, it was the pesky pocket gopher. Several hours later we checked the traps and found we had caught two gophers. Taking a roll of light twine and the two dead rodents, we walked to the barn, where Dad fastened a line to each of the gophers and laid the rodents in some tall grass. Then we returned to the house, unreeling the lines as we went.

At dusk we all seated ourselves comfortably in chairs on the back porch and waited for the owls to appear. It was uncanny how quietly

20

they could arrive. One moment the barn roof was empty, the next an owl was there. We all waited breathlessly to see what would happen. Dad took one of the strings and gave it a twitch. Instantly the owl stiffened and studied the ground intently. Slowly Dad inched the dead rodent out into the open. The owl watched a moment longer and then plummeted to the ground and pounced on the gopher. A moment later it took off, breaking the string, and landed with its prize in a nearby tree. It had really worked! Our doubts that we could fool an owl with a dead rodent had been stilled.

Moments later another owl appeared and the procedure was repeated. This time, however, Dad continued to pull the string slowly after the owl had caught the gopher. For several yards the surprised owl thrashed and grappled with the gopher that wouldn't die. Finally the string broke and the victorious owl flew away with his well-earned prize. We were all excited at the experience. Next night, my father promised, my sister and I could pull the string.

In those days of no television, this was the early show for the family. It became a nightly series sponsored by the local gopher population. Word spread of the good hunting by the barn, and soon several owls were waiting in the wings for the show to start. It soon became necessary to have four or five strings in order for everyone to have a chance.

Pulling a dead rodent with a string doesn't sound particularly exciting at first impression. But when we tried to outwit or outma-

Pocket gophers were his favorite food.

Kent's sister, Patsy, makes friends.

neuver the owl, it became a challenge. There were several variations. One was to see who in the family could get his gopher the farthest before the owl caught it. This required a quick hand and sharp eyes. If the owl looked away a moment, a quick tug on the string would gain a foot or more. Another variation was to see who could pull the owl the farthest before it broke the string. The trick here was to pull inches at a time, just enough to keep the owl off balance, but not hard enough to break the string.

A third variation was to try to make the owl miss the gopher. This was the most fun because it required critical timing. At the last instant, just before the owl made contact with the rodent, one had to give a quick jerk. If the timing was right, the owl would hit empty ground, a bit bewildered. In an instant, however, it would be after the target again. We could never make an owl miss the second time.

The feeling of a wild owl struggling and tugging on the end of the line was real excitement. It was an experience very much like having a fighting game fish on the end of a fishing line. The satisfying thing was that the "fish" was unharmed, and you could catch the same one over and over. "Owling" became a favorite pastime for our family and provided us with firsthand observations of how owls hunt. We noticed that sound was as much a factor as sight. A slight rustle in the grass would draw the owls' attention as quickly as the sight of the prey. The combination of sight and hearing makes the owl one of the most effective devices for rodent control in nature.

After these experiences it was no wonder that an owlet was to become the next family pet. Next spring found us raising a baby horned owl. At first he was only a white, downy bundle, about three-fourths yellow eyes, it seemed. For the first few days this tiny creature intimidated the whole family by clacking his beak fiercely whenever we approached. Gradually he began to accept food from our hands.

As the owlet grew he became firmly attached to his foster family.

Afternoon sunbathing.

Being of nocturnal nature, he provided fascinating entertainment in the evening in our living room. When he gained his prowess of flight, we exposed him to the outdoors and let him have the run of the place.

The most amazing thing about owls is their silent flight. Their wings produce almost no noise as they flap. Our owl was soon flying around the premises with ease. One disconcerting thing was that one could never hear him coming and his favorite perches were the heads of humans. It didn't matter whose head. It was startling, to say the least, when the first indication that the owl was near was its talons touching one's head. He was as gentle as possible, and for those of us who had hair there was no problem. Dad's head, however, had for some years been sparse in the hair department. As a matter of fact, it was quite slippery. Nevertheless, the owl never gave up trying to make it a perch; consequently, Dad's dome was constantly decorated with unintentional scratches.

By midsummer our tame owl could hoot as well as the wild ones, and often a chorus of owls would serenade us all night long, with our pet leading them from our rooftop. He loved companionship and often joined us on our afternoon walks by flying ahead and waiting for us to catch up. Usually at suppertime he would appear at the screen door and hang by his talons from the screen while peering into the kitchen. Once we let him in, he would immediately take up a position on the back of a chair and wait for tidbits. Cheese was his favorite snack.

In the warmth of the midday sun he could often be found sunning himself in the back yard. If my little sister, Patsy, was near, he usually joined her. He loved to bite at her long hair. Surely this night dweller that few people ever see is a most delightful citizen of the wild.

These early years of my life were filled with many experiences with the creatures of the wild. Whether they were wild or tamed, they provided me with firsthand knowledge of animals and birds which proved to be invaluable to me in later life. I shall always cherish the memories of those years. The moist, menthol smell of the eucalyptus forest on a foggy morning lingers on till this day. And I am certain that now, as then, the deep booming of the great horned owl still echoes through the forest.

Thirty years later, great horned owls are still a favorite subject.

2

A SUMMER AT
CANNERY ROW

The time came when we had to leave our isolated home in the woods because of my father's occupation—he was a commercial pilot engaged in aerial fish spotting for the fishing fleet. When I was twelve years old we moved some two hundred miles up the California coast to the small harbor town of Moss Landing.

In contrast to our other home, this one was in town. We lived right at the harbor, in a small house on the beach. The environment was new and different, to say the least: from the quiet of the forest to the bustle of a busy harbor. Instead of the deep hoots of the horned owls, we lived with the incessant bellow of the foghorn. But it was an exciting place for a twelve-year-old. Here, also, were youngsters of my own age, and before long I had many new friends.

Life in Moss Landing centered around fishing. Men worked on fishing boats, women worked in fish canneries, and boys fished from just about anywhere. From morning till night during the summer I practiced this new sport—out on the pier, from the beach, in the harbor, and even in the fish hoppers of the canneries. We boys seldom had money to buy new fishing gear, so our equipment consisted of things we found. Often it was some nylon line found twisted up in kelp on the beach, or hooks and sinkers pulled off the pier pilings at low tide. A forgotten jackknife found on the deserted pier at evening and a discarded tackle box completed my equipment.

Out on the pier I spent many hours lying face down by one of the many large holes in the old planking, through which I could watch my line as large perch swam right past my bait. Seldom did I get a bite, but on many occasions I snagged one of the large fish. Usually one or more of my friends were with me, fishing at different holes. One foggy morning my friend Joey came over to me excitedly to tell me about the huge perch he had almost caught. As he talked he took a few steps backward and vanished before my eyes. It took me a second to realize that he had fallen through a hole. Rushing up to the spot, I peered below to see him clinging to a barnacle-covered piling, yelling for all he was worth. I yelled to some fishermen nearby and then ran a block to a store to get a rope. I returned with it breathlessly, feeling like some kind of hero, only to find that the fishermen had already pulled Joey out.

The pier not only provided us with fishing spots, but proved to be a financial aid as well. Each morning big purse seiners returned to the harbor to unload their catch of sardines for the canneries. We discovered that the skippers could be persuaded to let a couple of small boys scramble over the deck, picking up fallen fish. In no time we each had a bucket full of fresh sardines and headed for the pier, where we peddled them at three for five cents for bait. A stop at the local store usually consumed our profits, as we bought ice cream and other such necessities.

The harbor was a natural estuary which had been deepened to accommodate vessels. The undredged portions extended for miles inland as a maze of meandering tideland waterways. This brackish backwater was a rich habitat for waterfowl and shore birds. Whenever we could commandeer a small rowboat, we set a course for this interesting place.

I thoroughly enjoyed rowing quietly along on a sunny afternoon, watching avocets and godwits probing the muddy banks. Often we would glide quietly past a great blue heron waiting patiently for a fish to pass within reach of its sharp beak. Terns, with their silver-white wings flashing, would dive headlong into the water for small fish. It was peaceful and fascinating to coast silently along and watch.

On my first trip up the slough I was startled to see a fin break water ahead and approach our skiff. In absolute fascination, I watched as a four-foot leopard shark glided past our skiff with its dorsal fin leaving a small wake on the glassy surface. It was the largest fish I had ever seen. I soon learned that the slough was alive with the sharks. In certain places at low tide it was impossible to row without hitting bodies with the oars. Much of our time was spent leaning over the prow of the skiff, watching the ghostly shapes swim by.

A few weeks later, we heard that a local fish buyer was paying ten cents a pound for leopard shark. The thought of such easy money brought fast action. We figured that just one of the monsters we had seen would weigh fifty pounds. Surely we could easily get three or four in a day. Nothing to it!

From previous experience we had discovered that our light tackle was useless on the large sharks, so we constructed a small make-shift harpoon fashioned after the large ones the local fishermen used to capture the thirty-foot basking sharks off the coast. Repeated honing soon gave our weapon a razor-sharp point. Throwing a length of light rope into a borrowed skiff and laying the six-foot harpoon rod across the bow, we set sail.

It was early morning when we rowed our way past the big commercial boats toward the slough. As we passed below the larger boats we gave the crew members a wave. We had a kinship with them now. If there was a snicker among the seasoned fishermen on the decks, it was well masked. We were embarking on a serious mission.

Once in the area, we began to row quietly and keep a sharp eye out. Up ahead a fin cut a wake on the glassy water. Joey stood up in the bow, harpoon at the ready, while I tried to bring us to the fish. Silently we coasted upon a big one, and Joey heaved a mighty throw. A clean miss! All morning we heaved the harpoon, until it was all bent out of shape. As we rowed our way home, past the commercial boats, we were aware of the eyes of the men on the decks. We secretly hoped they wouldn't ask us how it had gone. Instead, we hoped that they would figure from the condition of the twisted harpoon rod that we had had a battle royal with one of the monsters. It was none of their business that the rod was bent from countless plunges into the muddy bottom and sunken logs. We would re-outfit and return.

The following day wasn't much better for the first several hours. Finally, toward midday, we approached our millionth shark and Joey heaved. It struck home, a solid hit! Instantly the water was boiling as the shark tried to escape. We made the line fast and I started rowing ashore. But rowing as hard as I could I still lost ground (or water) to the shark. Little by little he pulled us out into deeper water. Then he tired and I almost made it ashore. But he got his second wind, and out we went again. Back and forth we went for fifteen minutes, water boiling, boys shouting. Finally Joey jumped the last five feet to shore. Once firmly footed, he was able to pull the thrashing fish ashore. A handy club subdued the monster, and we stood there winded and victorious. It was a big one, to be sure, a real shark almost five feet long with rows of sharp teeth. We were elated. Probably weighed fifty pounds. Five dollars! Wow!

The return trip to the harbor seemed excruciatingly slow. Passing the commercial boats, we tried to give them a casual wave. Our shark was carefully laid out in the bottom of the skiff so as to show off his full length. There was a gratifying whistle of admiration from up on the decks. We were one of 'em now.

A hundred yards more and we were at the fish buyer's dock. We found him in his dingy office working over some figures. He recognized us from before and grinned, revealing a mouthful of yellow-stained teeth. I thought they were absolutely the dirtiest teeth I had ever seen.

"Watcha kids got?" he questioned.

"You still buying shark for ten cents a pound, mister?" we asked.

"Every chance I get." Another yellow grin.

"O.K., then weigh this one," we said proudly.

He did, and it tipped the scales at thirty-eight pounds. We almost had the money spent when he informed us that he couldn't buy just *one* fish. He had to buy at least five hundred pounds at a time. This one shark wasn't worth anything. We walked away thoroughly discouraged with the shark fishing business.

Around this time, my father acquired two baby red-tailed hawks for us. Even with plenty to do around the harbor I had missed having a pet, and Dad and I had always wanted to train a hawk. These youngsters were white and downy, with large yellow feet. We prepared a box of soft grass for their temporary nest and put it in the kitchen. For the first few days their eyes were riveted on us and their mouths were constantly agape.

Dad purchased a chunk of horsemeat at a pet store and, with a large pair of scissors, cut off a small piece and offered it to one of the chicks. At first it recoiled in fear and refused the food. Dad showed me how to gently force open the hooked beak and put a piece of meat into the mouth. After a few minutes the chick swallowed the morsel. Another followed, until both hawks were fed. With their crops full, they lay down in their nest and promptly dropped off to sleep. We covered the box and quietly left the room.

We had often wanted to train a hawk in the art of falconry. We had read several books on the subject and felt it would be an exciting hobby. It is an ancient sport that began in Persia four thousand years ago. During the Middle Ages in Europe it became the sport of nobility. There was even a hierarchy among the various species of falcons and hawks set up by the noblemen. The fastest and most courageous species were reserved for the highest noblemen. The lower in rank a nobleman, the lower-class the hawk allowed him. At the bottom of the list was the kestrel, or sparrow hawk, a small falcon capable of catching only large insects and small birds.

Red-tailed hawks like ours didn't even place among nobility. They were considered much too slow and dull for the dashing noble-men. Nevertheless, we were proud of our hawks. We gave them all the careful attention a king would give his peregrine falcon. Each day we weighed the amount of food each bird received. They had to be fed exactly the right amount, not too little, not too much. The secret in training hawks is through their diet.

As my hawk grew older I began to train him to ride on my gloved arm. It was quite a thrill when he could ride the glove, standing erect and alert. I was very proud. I named him Buster, because I thought he would be a tough little hunter. This was wishful thinking, as I later discovered.

I was the envy of my friends as I walked up and down the paths of the fishing village with my "fierce hunter" riding confidently on my arm. To questions from young admirers I would reply with an air of pride that Buster was a trained hunting hawk; he would attack anything at my command. At this the younger ones would cringe away, but the bolder ones would urge me on so that they could see. I usually replied that it was far too dangerous to fly him around kids. In reality, Buster wouldn't hurt a flea. In fact, I was worried that he would never gain the desire and courage to attack even the smallest prey.

What Buster lacked in aggressiveness he made up for in looks. He was a handsome bird who enjoyed the company of people. In the side yard I built a perch where he could be fastened with a three-foot leash. The leash was attached to the short leather jesses which were fastened to his legs. The hawk soon learned that he was tied to the perch and resigned himself to it. On warm days he would lie down on the sand and spread his wings fully. In this position he appeared dead, and the first time I saw him sunning I was sure someone had killed him.

Each day Dad and I would give our birds their lesson. It consisted of tying a piece of meat to a padded horseshoe and coaxing the hawk to fly to this line for his meal. We always flew the hawks on a line to prevent their getting away before they were trained.

Kent with Buster.

Dad's hawk was an aggressive, boisterous bird. It could never wait for him to throw the line and often tried to take it from his hand before he was ready. Buster, however, was a different story. He had very little interest in the line. Food to him was a thing he could take or leave.

By the time Dad's hawk was flying free, mine had barely shown interest in the lure. I figured Dad's hawk was in the sixth grade and mine was in the second. Two or three times a week we took our hawks out into the country where there were large open fields. There I flew Buster on a line a few yards to the lure, while Dad's hawk circled high overhead, calling excitedly for him to throw the lure. At the first sight of the lure his hawk would plummet earthward to grapple fiercely with the padded horseshoe. There were even times when Dad's hawk took the lure away from Buster.

The day finally came when I decided to fly Buster free for the first time. After I launched him, he climbed to an altitude of two hundred feet and circled. I whistled, yelled, and whirled the lure vigorously, but he didn't even notice. Completely absorbed in his new freedom, he couldn't have cared less about the lure. After several minutes he landed atop a power pole and proceeded to preen his feathers. We knew it would be a long wait, so Dad went home while I kept the vigil. I lay back on the grass and looked skyward at my truant hawk.

This was the first of many times when I would be forced to wait out Buster's decisions on whether to come down or not. Much as I wanted him to respond to the lure, I nevertheless could sympathize with him. After all, it was much more interesting being on a power pole watching the surroundings than being home in his cage; and I have to admit I rather enjoyed those afternoons of lying flat on my back in a warm field. Every half hour I would try the lure again, with no luck. Buster would watch with interest as I whirled it around and around and tossed it twenty feet. For several minutes he would twist his head and look it over closely, but then he always returned to his former state of disinterest.

Frequently his return to me was not the result of the lure at all. Several times wild hawks pestered him with such persistence that Buster was forced lower and lower until he actually made a forced landing on the ground. I was always close behind and wasted no time in thrusting the lure at him. With the temptation of food just inches before his face he finally would react and hungrily gulp it down while I attached the leash.

Two miles down the coast from our house was an isolated area of sage-covered sand dunes. These dunes were a half-mile wide and several miles long, with the ocean on one side and farm fields on the other. No trees, no power poles, a perfect place to fly Buster. So this became our place. Nearly every day I would take hawk on glove and, with a pack containing my lunch and Buster's, walk along the beach to the dunes. There I'd climb the highest dune and place Buster on a sage branch. I'd disconnect his leash and we would sit together and survey the hillside below. These were the times when I enjoyed Buster the most. Often I would get close and talk to him, and it seemed at that moment he understood. We would often see cottontail rabbits hopping below and I'd talk softly, trying to encourage him to attack the rabbit. It wasn't malicious talk. It was encouragement for him to fulfill his role as a predator, and, of course, there was a desire on my part to be proud of his achievement. I knew that until he learned the skill of hunting he would be helpless should he ever decide to fly away. "Go on," I'd say, "you can do it." Just when I thought he was ready to attack he would turn to me and bite at my hair or nibble my ear. Once again I was disappointed. My hawk was a pacifist!

There was a day, however, when he did see something that interested him. Off he went, slicing down the hill, disappearing behind a bush. I followed pell-mell down the hill, leaping over sage, and arrived breathlessly, fully expecting to see Buster standing proudly on his prey. Imagine my disappointment when I found him watching very closely the progress of a beetle across the sand. With a chirp of welcome he hopped to my arm, leaving the beetle unmolested.

Once, when Dad and I were at the dunes together, Dad caught a live field mouse with his hands. "Bring your hawk," he said. "We're going to teach him to catch a mouse."

In an open area I readied my hawk on my fist. I knelt down as Dad turned the mouse loose a scant two feet in front of Buster. In order to get him to leave the fist I literally pulled my glove from beneath him. Suddenly he found himself on the ground face to face with a live mouse. We stood back to see what would happen. Slowly Buster leaned over and, with his beak, tried to touch the mouse, gently so as not to hurt it. Then, of all things, the mouse bit Buster and hung on to his lower bill. Frantically the distraught hawk dashed around with his "prey" hanging on for dear life. Finally the whole ridiculous affair ended when the mouse let go and made a well-deserved break for the brush. I was humiliated and crushed. My fierce hunter attacked by a mouse! Who would ever believe it! I was glad Dad was the only witness; he would keep the secret. I knew then that I would never have a hunter. I would have to be satisfied with a companion.

There is a certain responsibility that one takes on in acquiring wild creatures for pets, especially hawks. Their diet is very important. Hawks must have meat every day, and at least twice weekly they must consume fur or feathers with the meat. The roughage is swallowed along with the meat and is later regurgitated after it has cleansed the bird's crop.

Hawks require a great amount of care and attention. A permit is required today to retain hawks for falconry, but the law requiring such permits is not enforced as it should be. Unless a youth is extremely responsible and conscientious, he should not attempt to raise hawks. So much time is required that most young people lose interest after a few weeks and release their birds completely unprepared for survival in the wild. An experience that I will relate is an example of what problems can arise if one becomes careless.

Our hawks spent much of the day on outdoor perches, but they were never left unattended. Any hawk that is tethered to a perch is quite helpless when pestered by dogs or children. In spite of our caution, an accident did happen. Probably due to a poor job of knot-tying on my part, Buster's leash came loose as he tried to fly off when a dog peered around the corner. I was horrified to see him winging his way across the harbor with three feet of leather leash trailing behind. In a few minutes he vanished across the slough a half mile away.

It was about two miles by road to the spot where we had last seen

Buster. Dad and I searched in vain through a grove of trees, scanned every power pole, all to no avail. We knew that there was very little chance that Buster would survive even one landing with all that leash hanging from him. Even now he was probably hanging from some branch, dying a slow death.

Since Dad had to return to work, I continued the search alone. I had hastily prepared a lure to coax Buster down if I found him alive. For several hours I wandered through the trees, looking up until my neck ached. Then I heard a distant sound of crows scolding. That was a good clue, since crows often mob perching hawks. I hurried toward the noise, arriving in minutes beneath a tall eucalyptus tree around which crows were buzzing like angry hornets. Sure enough, there was Buster about midway up the tree, nervously watching the crows. With so much activity around, he scarcely noticed me. My joy at finding him was short-lived when I realized there was absolutely no way I could get him. My tossing of the lure was a feeble attempt to attract his attention.

The rising crescendo of the crow mob was getting to him. Crow-watching was fun to a point, but this was a bit ridiculous. He began to look nervously around and presently launched off the branch. His leash snagged briefly on a limb, my heart stopped, but then he broke free and sailed off in a southerly direction.

Frantically I ran after him, yelling futilely, trying desperately to keep him in sight. He was headed toward a series of steel high-voltage power poles. To my horror he landed on one of the towers. I ran up and repeated the useless act of tossing the lure. I knew before I tossed it that it wouldn't work. But I had to do something.

He wasn't satisfied with this perch and was about to fly again. In a moment he took off, snagged again, and hung upside down for agonizing seconds before breaking loose. I was weak and shaky from the close call, but I hurried after him. His next landing site was right in the midst of a complex of electric towers that carried high-voltage lines directly out of the plant. In this dangerous and unlikely spot Buster settled down with apparent satisfaction.

I was heartsick and on the verge of tears when Dad arrived later in the day. When I pointed to the figure of Buster perched dangerously amid all that high voltage, Dad uttered a low moan and declared that Buster was done for. He told me to wait while he went back home for something.

Twenty minutes later he returned with his rifle. He explained that when Buster got hung up he would shoot him rather than have him suffer a slow death. Together we waited and watched. I longed to have my hawk safely back, but at this point it didn't look very hopeful. We planned to stay until dark and be certain Buster was settled for the night.

In the late afternoon a pickup truck with the power company sign on its door arrived. A stern-looking man with hard hat greeted us coldly.

"That your hawk up there?" He gestured toward the tower.

"Yes," answered Dad.

"Name and address?" he asked curtly.

"Why?" Dad asked.

"Well, that tower carries several hundred thousand volts of electricity. If that hawk falls across those wires, it'll blow a transformer. Them transformers ain't cheap. We want to know who to charge."

Dad gulped as he gave name and address.

The man left without saying another word. As soon as he had gone, Dad reached into the car, got the rifle, loaded it, and walked toward the tower.

"What are you going to do?" I cried. I didn't want him to shoot Buster, but it seemed the only thing to do. Through the binoculars we could see that the leash was tangled around the steel framework. He didn't have a chance.

Dad braced himself against the tower and sighted carefully. For long, agonizing moments I stood with head turned away, tears in my eyes, waiting for the shot. But there was no shot. I turned.

Dad lowered the gun. "I'm afraid that if I shoot now he'll fall across the wire and blow the transformer anyhow," he said. "We'll wait."

I breathed a sigh. Buster was reprieved.

Darkness came, and Buster's stay of execution was further extended. In the dark we knew he wouldn't move. We made our way home. Dinner was a quiet affair. I could hardly eat. Dad said we would

A "not so tough" hawk.

get up before daylight and return to the tower. I prepared a lure with fresh meat, making it look as enticing as possible. I prayed that Buster would get to eat it.

Before dawn we were in position at the tower. The morning was wet and foggy. Fog dripped from trees and tower. High-voltage power lines snapped and crackled in the dampness. As dawn slowly arrived the tower loomed before us. The cold steel braces cut a crisp outline in the fog at the base but melted into the mist at the top. From the harbor the mournful moan of the foghorn completed the weird scene. Somewhere at the invisible top sat Buster, we hoped.

Finally the fog lifted enough to reveal the form of Buster, thoroughly soaked but still in the same position. I walked into a clearing and called to him. Dad followed with the rifle. Moments later Buster gave signs of preparing to fly. The moment of truth had arrived. I watched with fear as the hawk launched from the steel tower. Within three feet he reached the end of the leash and was snapped down across a high-voltage wire. There was a loud pop, a puff of smoke—and Buster flew free!

We could hardly believe it. Nearly all of the leash remained securely fastened to the tower. For some reason he hadn't been electrocuted. Buster sailed a half mile farther and landed on another tower. But now he didn't have the full leash to bother him. We were thankful for that. But we still had to get him down.

I was sure that he must be starved by now, so once again I tossed the lure. Then, lo and behold, down he came, straight for the lure. Well, almost. In a beautiful dive he plummeted to the ground ten feet from the lure. I rushed over to find that Buster had come down to a caterpillar! While he stood face to face with the peculiar-looking creature I attached the leash. My wayward hawk was safely home.

Later when we examined the remains of the leash we found that it had been burned to a crisp up to a point three inches from his legs. We figured the electricity had traveled as far as the leash was damp. Buster's feathers had kept the last three inches dry and thus saved his life. We never heard from the power company, so apparently no damage was done. Buster was a very lucky hawk. After this experience I was much more careful in attaching the leash to the perch.

From this time on Buster grew to be a powerful hunter of all creeping and crawling things. Nothing was too small for him. Even ladybugs were pursued with great persistence. Somehow Buster never did develop a strong desire to come to the lure. No matter how I dressed the lure up to make it look appetizing, it didn't interest him if he had to come any distance. Consequently, I spent many hours beneath trees, poles and other unreachable perches, waiting for Buster to decide he was hungry enough to come down.

In spite of the obvious fact that Buster was no well-trained hunter, I had thoroughly enjoyed his company all summer, walking with him on the fist, chasing him across country or simply waiting for him beneath a lofty perch. But summer was coming to an end. Mother, my sister and I were moving south to Carpinteria, where I would start high school. Dad would remain in Moss Landing to finish the fishing season and then would join us. I decided to leave Buster with Dad so that he could be flown occasionally.

Before dawn one morning we left. I went to Buster's cage and looked in. With a lump in my throat I said a last goodbye. He turned and uttered a few sleepy peeps. Then he tucked his head into his feathers and returned to sleep. I closed the flap and left. I never saw Buster again. Several weeks later while he was flying at the sand dunes he followed a wild hawk away. I like to think that Buster had a long life feeding on caterpillars and grasshoppers and other such elusive prey.

3

THE BLACK RAIDER

The next four years passed rapidly and without the usual array of pets. I attended a boarding high school and was home only a few weekends during the school year. Studies became a more serious thing now, and I began to realize that the natural-science courses were of special interest to me.

Upon entering Loma Linda University at Riverside, California, I began a four-year study that would lead to a bachelor's degree in biology. In studying biology I learned why animals and birds behave the way they do. I was able to understand some of the behavior I had observed in the wildlife I had come in contact with over the years.

The desert and hills around the college provided the biology students with a rich habitat for field study. There were always a few students who carried this field study to extremes. One of my best friends was a snake enthusiast. Although the dorm rules forbade pets in the room, this dedicated student of herpetology devised schemes to import reptiles. It seemed that only the largest and most deadly snakes were desirable. Trips to the nearby deserts reaped a harvest of diamondback rattlesnakes and sidewinders that would put a zoo to shame. His room soon became a hodgepodge of cages placed in every convenient and not-so-convenient place. Electric cords were strung around the room like spaghetti so that each cage would have a light for warmth. Frequent raids were made on the biology labs, which netted him assorted rats and mice intended for lab experiments. These rodents seldom lasted until morning in a cage with a large red diamondback rattlesnake.

On special occasions word was spread through the dorm underground that Ron was going to stage a demonstration of his snakes. Soon the room would be crammed, and, as everyone watched intently, he would extract a four-foot red diamondback. The demonstration usually consisted of no more than putting the reptile on the floor and letting it slither toward the onlookers. This usually prompted a leap by everyone to the bed, the dresser or anything else that would support a human body. After repeating this with his entire menagerie, Ron would announce that the show was over.

My tastes didn't include reptiles. I had a variety of small creatures that, for one reason or another, were given to me to care for. Sparrow hawks seemed to be the birds most often captured by youngsters in the area, and they always ended up in my custody. There was a screech owl that someone had found standing in the middle of the road one night. When it was brought to me the owl appeared to be stunned, but it stood perfectly on my desk with eyes open, looking for all the world like a mounted specimen. Only an occasional blink of an eye showed life. By the next day he had recovered, and toward dusk I released him in a thick grove of trees.

The most demanding creature I had in college was a raven. My roommate and I lived off campus in a small apartment, and we each decided to have a raven for a pet. At first the two ravens we acquired were small and not too vociferous. But this lasted only briefly. As they grew, so did their voices and their demands for food. Their screeches became incessant and their red mouths were constantly open, waiting for someone to throw something, anything, into the cavernous depths. Canned dogfood was cheapest. With a spoon we'd flip a gob down each throat. There would be a gurgled interruption in the squawking and the food would vanish.

The problem was that, although both Bob and I took turns at racing back to the apartment between classes, the ravens never got their fill. One day our landlord inquired somewhat hesitantly about the constant squawking sounds from our apartment. We suddenly realized that should the noise continue he would want to investigate further. The thought of the landlord seeing the inside of our apartment brought visions of instant eviction.

The ravens were no longer confined to the box they had originally arrived in. They were quite mobile now, using wings, feet and even beak to clamber about the apartment. The apartment, as one might expect, was not in the best order. Ravens have never been noted for their cleanliness. At first we tried covering the furniture with papers, but somehow they never stayed put. We finally gave up, in favor of hastily cleaning up the mess when we fed the birds. Hardly a spot in the room escaped the ravens.

One of their favorite perches was atop the lamp. If they perched on opposite sides at the same time, things balanced out pretty well. But if both decided to sit on one side, over they went. We took to laying the lamp on its side on the floor before we left.

We thought of confining the ravens to one room, but, since the only room that had a door was the bathroom, we decided against it. The bathroom window opened directly toward the landlord's living-room window. That would be asking for trouble, we thought. It became obvious that we had to find a way to silence our pets' infernal squawks for food.

It was fortunate that, at the time, I was courting a lovely young lady whom I had met in the college library. Tall, dark-haired, beautiful, with a vivacious personality, Judi had another trait that held a special appeal for me under the circumstances: she had a great desire to be of help. It wasn't hard to persuade her to help us with the ravens.

I explained that our ravens needed to be fed at the eleven- and two-o'clock period breaks. Bob and I had lab at that time. She agreed to go to the apartment that afternoon for some on-the-job training.

As we approached, the usual din of the ravens became louder. When we entered, the first thing Judi saw was the red throat of a raven thrust at her from the arm of a chair. She recoiled slightly, but soon regained her composure. I cautioned her not to sit anywhere. One glance told her why. I tried to ignore her wrinkled nose as she looked about the room.

I showed her how to scoop up a gob of dogfood and flip it down a waiting throat. After several tries she finally mastered the art of a

The handkerchief thief.

direct hit on the gaping mouth. From then on, for several weeks, this most willing young lady could be seen dashing across campus twice daily to toss gobs of food at bottomless throats. After that somewhat distasteful experience it is surprising that she agreed to become my wife. Since that time, Judi has been a willing helper with many of my wild pets.

At the end of the school year I took Hey Boy—my raven—home with me. My parents now lived in the country near Santa Barbara, California. There on the ranch he learned to fly and became the local nuisance. He was allowed to fly free and seemed to take it as his solemn duty to keep things stirred up as much as possible.

The family cat was a constant target of his raucous calls and dive-bomb attacks. But people were his favorite victims. He took great delight in perching on the roof and waiting for someone to step from the house. Then he would swoop down and deliver a sharp

44

peck to the head of the unsuspecting victim. And the louder the victim yelled, the better Hey Boy liked it. Another favorite target was toes—women's toes. It was the fashion at that time for women to wear toeless shoes. These were extremely fascinating to Hey Boy. New visitors didn't realize what he was doing when he hopped up to their feet. To all appearances he was only admiring their shoes. In reality he was singling out the ones with the most toe exposure. Then, with rapid staccato jabs, he would run his screaming victim into the house —the louder the better.

Hey Boy's career almost came to an end as a result of his constant pestering of his victims. This time his target was a golden eagle, named Lady, that we had for many years. Lady flew the property quite frequently, and Hey Boy resented her intrusion on his air space. He would set out with a vengeance to defend his property. Often his quick dives surprised the eagle, and on several occasions he actually caused her to crash into the ground. It was obvious to us that Hey Boy's days were numbered if he continued such dangerous activity.

One day the eagle was flying about the property when Hey Boy made one of his surprise attacks. Lady was caught near the ground,

Hey Boy doing what he is best at . . . pestering visitors.

and, in the process of trying to outmaneuver the black attacker, she crashed. Hey Boy swooped jubilantly up to a perch and directed a tirade at the eagle. Lady was getting a little hot under the collar by this time. It was bad enough to be outmaneuvered, but to be jeered about it from the rooftop was too much.

Once again she took to the air. Hey Boy watched as she circled out over the valley. He carefully planned his next attack. As the eagle swooped in low, Hey Boy launched himself from the rooftop and bore down on her with fanatical eagerness. Just as he reached Lady, she rolled over into an inverted position and lashed out with a huge taloned foot. There was a hoarse squawk from Hey Boy as the two birds hit the ground in a jumble of black feathers. The yellow foot of the eagle had found its mark and now held the black protester helpless in its grasp. Just as she was about to deliver the *coup de grâce* to the raven, Dad rushed up with a broom and separated them. Hey Boy took to the air somewhat shakily and returned to his perch, where he remained quietly the rest of the day. Never again did he pester Lady.

Just as people have their daily routine, so do other creatures. Hey Boy had a routine that seldom varied from day to day. Each morning after being fed he promptly began a large circuit that would hit all points of interest and eventually bring him home several hours later. We knew of his wanderings but were unaware of the specifics of his appointments on this circuit until reports drifted in from surrounding farms. Little by little we were able to piece together Hey Boy's activities from these eyewitness reports.

The first stop after the morning meal at home was the Parsons farm directly down the hill from us. There he announced his arrival with a few loud calls designed to stir things up a bit. If there were no cats or dogs immediately available to pester, he went to the chicken pens. He could usually count on a snack of a fresh egg that some uneducated hen had laid outside on the ground. If no hen eggs were available he always made an attempt to flush one of the mallards off its nest. If this failed, he would fling a few disgusted caws over his black shoulder and flap off to his next stop.

One of his favorite stops was the small airport nearby. Air traffic was usually very light, and many days Hey Boy was the only aircraft landing there. There were usually a couple of helicopter pilots who were on standby to fly to the offshore oil rigs. These men grew fond of Hey Boy's visits and always had a snack for the black raider.

One morning before Hey Boy arrived, a small plane landed at the airport. After getting some fuel, the pilot spread out his air map on the back of the fuselage and began to study it intently. While he was engrossed in his study Hey Boy arrived and landed on a nearby pole to study the situation. Then quietly he swooped in and landed on the tail of the aircraft. Still the pilot didn't see him. Then Hey Boy plopped down to the fuselage, walked up to the map, and calmly grabbed a corner with his beak. At that moment the pilot turned and stared wide-eyed at the raven. Hey Boy pulled, but the pilot hung on. Not a word was spoken. Finally the pilot laid his arm across the map to hold it and tried to ignore the pesky raven, as if this were just one of the hazards of making cross-country flights. After several minutes of tugging, Hey Boy flew off to his next stop.

At the farm up the road, Hey Boy could always count on a good reaction from the dog. To announce his arrival Hey Boy would usually make a surprise attack as the poor, unsuspecting animal slept near the drive. If he was quick enough he could get in a good peck before Fido even knew he was around. Once he had the dog's attention, he led him on a merry chase around the farm, always keeping just out of reach. Predictably, the dog would finally collapse in a heap and stare glassy-eyed at his tormenter. Hey Boy usually had one last trick to complete the dog's humiliation; the Japanese owner of the farm observed this bit of trickery on several occasions.

Around the farm were a number of terraced areas where the ground sloped off steeply three or four feet to another level. Frequently Hey Boy would land at the edge of one such terrace and pretend to be interested in something on the ground. In spite of his exhaustion, the dog could not resist the temptation presented by the preoccupied raven just out of reach. Summoning up his last reserve of strength, the dog would charge the last few feet toward the raven, confident that victory was his. With perfect timing, Hey Boy would leap straight up out of reach, while the poor dog hurtled off the terrace to end in a tumble at the bottom. The jeering calls of Hey Boy only added to the dog's humiliation. Fun over, Hey Boy headed off in another direction.

There were many more stops along the way, some only a few minutes, others an hour or more, depending on the action. Finally, in late afternoon, he would arrive again at home, mission completed.

It was certain that sooner or later Hey Boy's wanderings would cause him trouble. He developed a great interest in the laundry that waved briskly from the lines of many of the farm homes. It intrigued him so much that he just had to do something about it. He began by collecting socks. At first the ladies took it good-naturedly, thinking one sock would satisfy him. Not so. This was a challenge to Hey Boy. It wasn't easy to twist a sock from the grasp of a clothespin. No matter how the women fastened the socks, however, Hey Boy always managed to pry them loose. And for some devilish reason he never took two of the same pair. The greatest fun in the whole game was to fly high over the orchard and drop the sock into the top of a lemon tree!

Time out for an omelet.

Needless to say, this habit was to be the downfall of Hey Boy. Word soon reached us that the local women were getting angry. Most of them refused to use their lines, especially when Hey Boy was perched on their rooftop, challenging them to hang one he couldn't get loose.

Finally sentence was passed on the black raider. After a solemn conference we decided that he should be transported for life. Dad put him, squawking and protesting, into a box. Once in the darkened box, Hey Boy became unusually quiet. It was as if he knew that the jig was finally up and something serious was about to happen. Dad strapped the box into the back seat of his plane and flew thirty miles out to sea to the small, uninhabited island of San Miguel. There, among many wild ravens, Hey Boy was released to live his outlaw life miles from humans. With a few loud caws he flew rapidly away, searching, no doubt, for the nearest laundry line.

4

AT HOME
WITH A HARE

Anyone who ever visits the arid deserts and foothills of the Southwest will sooner or later come into contact with one of its most common residents, the jackrabbit. Several species of these animals thrive in the dry regions. Although commonly called rabbits, they are actually hares, distinguished from rabbits by having long hind legs for leaping and extremely long, broad ears. Nocturnal by habit, they seldom venture out during the daylight hours, but emerge under cover of darkness to graze on dry grasses and desert shrubs. In rural areas it is not uncommon to see a dozen or more jackrabbits feeding under the stars in grassy schoolyards or on golf courses. A drive along a desert road at night will often flush one or more jacks into bounding gracefully off at speeds of up to 45 miles per hour.

Since the college I attended was in the desert, jackrabbits were numerous on and off campus. Although I had never had close contact with the large hares, I always admired their incredible mobility.

Much to my disgust, I learned that one of the favorite pastimes of some of my fellow students was to drive to a nearby alfalfa field and shoot rabbits at night. To them it was great sport to slaughter the animals as they sat blinded in the headlights of several cars, and they sometimes killed as many as fifty or sixty animals in a single night. It was true, as they said, that there was an excess of rabbits around, and that the population should be kept down. But no one seemed to be aware that the reason the rabbits were multiplying so fast was that their natural predators such as hawks, coyotes, and bobcats had also been hunted by sportsmen.

It was on a night field trip with my field biology class that I had my first contact with the "jackass" rabbit. On a desolate desert road a jack burst from the brush and bounded gracefully ahead of our vehicle. For several hundred yards he sprinted, and then he veered off the trail and stopped. In the glare of the spotlight he froze and crouched low.

A few in our group had guns and began blazing away at the hapless hare. Fortunately, although the animal was only fifty yards away, no one could hit him. After several volleys of ineffective fire they paused to express their feelings.

At this opportune moment I grabbed a butterfly net and began a careful approach toward the immobile rabbit. Skeptical laughter came from the truck as I stalked my prey. No doubt it was a ridiculous sight in the glare of the lights on the stark desert floor.

The rabbit remained crouched as I crept within ten feet, my net at the ready. Step by step I moved forward, until I stood only three feet away. No sound from the truck now. With a quick movement I brought the net down on the rabbit. This contact woke him from his trance, and straight up he went—out of the net and ten feet away in one bound. Then suddenly he stopped, confused by the lights and his own eerie shadow. He turned and hopped rapidly toward me. I made a wild swing, to which the rabbit responded by darting between my legs. Now things were getting exciting. He went in and out of my legs while I swung madly to and fro with the net. Around and around he went, always barely escaping my net but never running away. There were cheers and applause from the truck now as the pace picked up.

In the total confusion of the moment the long shadows of the rabbit, myself, and the arching net created an eerie psychedelic pattern on the desert floor. Finally, in a brilliant accidental move, I netted my prey. There were shouts of approval from the truck, and the class raced over.

I held the frightened animal securely while everyone got a good look. For all of us it was our first close look at a live jackrabbit. The delicate pattern of the blood vessels in his huge ears was particularly interesting. Not wanting to cause the unfortunate creature any more discomfort, I asked for the lights to be turned away, and after a few moments I released him. For several seconds he remained in the same position, inanimate as a desert rock. Then someone moved and in a flash he was gone, bounding back into the comfort of darkness. There was a satisfaction on my part, and I believe the other class members shared it, that a life hadn't been snuffed out for selfish pleasure. We had captured the prey and released him unharmed. It was this pacifist attitude toward animals that eventually led me into motion-picture filming of wildlife. Here I could satisfy my desire for a closer experience with animals without destroying them.

I finished college with a Bachelor's degree in biology, married Judi and established our home in Ventura, about fifty miles from my parents. During this period I began my apprenticeship as a motion-picture photographer, filming a golden eagle my father and I had trained. Dad and I both learned to handle the camera and gained valuable experience filming the eagle.

Several years after my college experience with jackrabbits I had the privilege of knowing one more closely.

My first filming assignment was for the *Lassie* television series. It was a story that I had suggested to them, involving a family of jackrabbits. Through this and later filming experiences I learned firsthand information about this desert dweller that so many people use merely as a target.

In order to raise a baby jackrabbit successfully one must obtain it at an early age, preferably just as it is able to hop about. One of the most interesting individuals I had was a male named, appropriately, Jack. He was found in an orchard, bewildered and confused, crouched in a naked furrow. He was no larger than a tennis ball when I adopted him.

Within a few hours he was successfully on the bottle, drinking until his tiny belly was tight as a drum. Feeding times were frequent, about every two hours for the first week, and bottle feedings became the motivating factor as I began filming. No matter where the bottle went, he was sure to follow. All I had to do was film while my assistant showed the bottle to Jack and then led him in the proper direction. Of course, I could add variation to the scene by leading

53

Judi and a young Jack.

him past various props or across difficult terrain. For example, a small eroded ditch would become a serious obstacle, a natural barrier, the Grand Canyon of the rabbit world. His efforts at getting around or across the canyon made interesting filming. A log in his path provided just the opposite kind of barrier. With an occasional sniff of the bottle he could be coaxed over the log, along it or through it, depending on the script. His was a fanatical obsession for the bottle, one which I used to the fullest.

Few animals in nature are more marvelously adapted for survival than the jackrabbit. It is a good thing, because he is tops on the desert predators' list of prey. His long legs, which appear rather awkward when he is young, provide incredible power and speed when he is full-grown. Speeds of forty-five miles an hour and leaps of twenty feet over the sage are not uncommon. Jackrabbits' large, bulbous brown eyes provide not only forward vision but good peripheral vision to the sides and above their line of sight.

Perhaps their most valuable asset is their huge ears. When erect the ears are sound reflectors, picking up the smallest sounds and transmitting them to the eardrum. They are swivel-mounted and can rotate like radar antennas to locate the sound source. A second function of the large ears is that of a cooling radiator. Each ear contains an intricate network of blood vessels that carry blood close to the surface. On a hot day the rabbit will sit in the shade with ears erect. Perspiration evaporating from the thin membrane cools the blood as it is pumped through the vessel network. Nature used the evaporative cooler for desert living long before man ever thought of it.

In spite of these survival modifications, the jackrabbit's life usually ends rather abruptly within the first two years. Predators, accidents or disease take their toll.

By the time Jack was half grown, with the gangly legs and tall erect ears that identified him as a jackrabbit, he had become the household pet and would follow anyone that moved. During the day he would usually doze in a small outdoor cage, but come nightfall he would rouse and look eagerly toward the house. His whole life was wrapped up in his evening romps in the house. For the family it was better than television.

These nightly sessions revealed a personality of the jackrabbit that could never be discovered by observing wild rabbits for a hundred years. In the house each evening Jack was at his absolute best. There was no apprehension, no fear, nothing to hamper his expressing his full character.

The most amazing characteristic of jackrabbits that we discovered in all of the dozen or so rabbits we raised over the years was their playfulness. In a species that is one of the most hunted of all creatures, one would think there wouldn't be a playful streak left. It is true that most of this play has a purpose—that of sharpening the animal's reflexes and escape techniques. There were things, however, that didn't appear to have any relationship to the role that the jackrabbit plays in nature as the prey.

Upon entering the house Jack would immediately check everything to make sure all was secure. Down the hall he would lope, poking into each bedroom and finally into my den. (I always spread down several sheets of newspaper, which he used fastidiously as a toilet. I don't know how he learned this, but he never failed to use the paper when he was in the house.) Then he would come out into the living room, sniffing each chair and piece of furniture. Once he was satisfied all was well, he began to loosen up.

Half grown as he was, he was in his prime. Lean and sinewy, he was the uncatchable prey. Sitting in the center of the living room, he would start his performance. With an instantaneous move he would spring straight up a foot or more, quivering like a fish, and streak out for the end of the hall. He loved the carpet because it gave him great traction. In the twenty-five feet to the end of the hall I am sure he reached twenty miles an hour, and I have never seen another animal that could stop and turn around as quickly as Jack. It was almost as if he were fastened by a rubber cord. A split second after he left the living-room floor he was back in exactly the same spot, nose quivering, ears erect, eyes wild.

He wasn't in a house with humans. He was in the desert, pitting his every faculty against his enemies. A coyote was ready to pounce. Or maybe a bobcat. With hind claws tearing at the carpet, Jack would rip off down the hall again. Often he would accelerate so fast that his front end would come clear of the floor and for a moment he would race on two legs. It was incredibly funny, and he seemed to enjoy our laughter. Frequently these mad dashes would be spiced up a little by a sharp zigzag or a kicking up of the heels as if to show that he had plenty of zip left.

As the evening progressed he extended his run into my den, through a bedroom, and back to the living room, all at high speed. The run down the hallway and back was fine, but it lacked something. He was a long-distance runner. He needed more room. We had tried to discourage him from entering the kitchen, but it was inevitable that sooner or later he would end up there and discover that the kitchen floor was a bit different from the carpet.

Sure enough, on one of his high-speed returns from the hall Jack decided to extend his runway. Without slowing down he rolled into a sharp turn and hit the smooth waxed floor of the family room and kitchen. There was instant confusion. He was all legs and ears as he skidded uncontrollably across the floor. His powerful hind legs were absolutely useless now. His claws, which provided him with such wonderful traction on the carpet, now behaved as if they were roller skates. A split second later there was a crash as he collided with the refrigerator. We all thought he would be killed or at least maimed for life. But he picked himself up, shook his head, and limped back toward the safety of the carpet. From that day on he had a healthy respect for the kitchen floor.

About mid-evening it was time for intermission and refreshments. Although he had outgrown the bottle, he never lost his love for milk and now drank from a bowl like a cat. He would consume the entire bowl in a single sitting, nibble on a snack of shredded wheat, and resume the show.

The performance after the intermission always possessed an added quality that really convulsed visitors with laughter. With his belly full of milk, his violent maneuvers were accompanied by loud sloshing sounds from within. It sounded like someone shaking a hot-water bag. It was very audible and one couldn't help wondering how he kept from churning the milk into butter.

We knew that the mad dashes and maneuvers were important for him to learn how to handle his equipment for later survival. But there was apparently no reason other than play that stimulated him to chase a ball. He didn't know what to do with it once he caught it, but he loved the chase.

Exploring the bookcase.

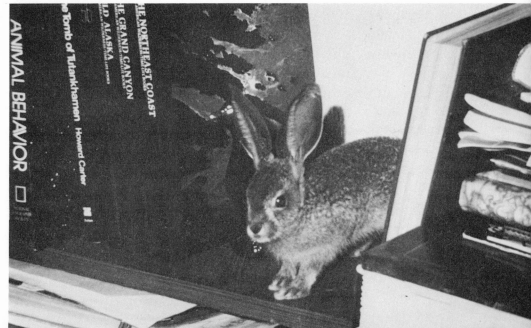

Another favorite game, or activity, was playing with a handkerchief that I flipped at him. If I flipped it at his paws and jerked it back he would pounce on it with his front paws with a vengeance. Since the front paws are jackrabbits' weapons when fighting other rabbits, this activity has its usefulness. Often he would get quite carried away and would hammer away at the handkerchief viciously while growling from deep within. Growling? Most people don't think of jackrabbits as having a voice, but they can vocalize when frightened or injured and will growl when fighting. I once observed a jackrabbit being pursued by a swooping golden eagle as it bounded through the sage. The rabbit's course took it in a huge circle and eventually brought it directly toward me. I sat immobile by a Joshua tree and watched as the eagle made another plunge not more than a hundred feet before me. As the eagle hovered momentarily a dozen feet above the rabbit, the hare began a series of violent figure-eight evasive maneuvers, each sharp turn sending geysers of desert sand into the air. All the while the animal was screaming like a human who was about to be murdered. Then the eagle dropped—and missed. The rabbit bounded safely away.

When Jack was nearly full grown we obtained a puppy for our children. The introduction of these two unlikely creatures on the living-room floor was quite a sight, since the rabbit was almost twice the size of the dog. What the pup lacked in size he made up for in noise. Jack was not going to be intimidated by the yaps of the pup, however, and was determined not to alter his routine. His mad dashes up and down the hall were often followed by the pup. Well, he tried, anyhow. The pup was not the fastest thing around, and by the time his brain had given the command to his legs to follow that rabbit, the rabbit was already back. The result was hilarious. The confused pup spent most of his time turning in circles, trying to keep the rabbit in view. If the pup happened to be in Jack's way, Jack simply sailed over him and was not above giving the pup a sharp kick from his midair position. Such physical contact usually sent the dog yelping beneath a chair.

As the pup grew older he grew braver and, of course, larger. By now Jack was an adult and was getting a bit short-tempered. The dog was no match for the rabbit and usually gave up after a brief chase. There was one place, however, where Jack was at a disadvantage—the kitchen floor. Jack had learned to tread softly on the floor and occasionally crossed it to another carpeted area on the far side. During the crossing, however, any sudden move on his part would send him sprawling.

On one of Jack's careful crossings, the pup recognized his opportunity and moved in. Jack lost his self-control and gave it all he had. With all four feet spinning like machinery, he made it to the center of the room under the table. There he took refuge on a small rug no more than four feet in diameter.

The rabbit was a prisoner on an island of traction in a sea of slick. The dog, realizing he had the upper hand for a change, tormented the rabbit (and us) with his ceaseless barking. Finally Jack could take no more. Gathering his powerful feet under him, he launched himself into the air, sailed over the slick floor, and landed right on the astounded dog. With a dozen sharp kicks of his hind feet Jack sent the dog tumbling head over heels. Needless to say, the dog learned the lesson well and was considerably quieter from then on.

My purpose in acquiring Jack was to film him, and, since I had gotten as much as I needed of him as a baby, I was now eager to film him as an adult, in his natural habitat, the desert. I was well aware of the difficulty of filming jackrabbits in the wild. They are extremely nervous. A crack of a twig can send them racing blindly for distant places. I assumed that I would lose Jack when I took him to the desert, but was hopeful of getting a few good shots before he took leave of me.

For this filming episode I planned carefully. I chose a remote part of the desert, where there was no danger from hunters. In order to contain Jack within range of my lens I constructed a large circular fence out of chicken wire and concealed it behind shrubs and bushes so as to enclose an area about a hundred feet in diameter. Such an enclosure is often necessary to keep tamed animals from wandering while filming. Within the compound was a variety of natural settings in which I could film the rabbit.

When everything was ready, I took Jack's cage from my truck

and set it within the compound. He eagerly sniffed the air and listened for strange sounds. This was his natural habitat, yet he had never known it. My fear was that he would charge full speed out of the cage, run headlong into the fence and be injured. Or at best he would clear the fence and be away in a flash.

For thirty minutes I let him familiarize himself with the surroundings from within the cage. Then, with the camera ready, I opened the cage door and stepped back. To my surprise he exited slowly and cautiously. While my camera hummed, he investigated every bush and sampled each kind of grass. For an hour he hopped leisurely about the compound, discovering the fence and its boundaries. This was the first time I was able to film a jackrabbit going about its natural behavior in a natural setting. Previous filming attempts with wild rabbits had netted me only shots of them racing frantically away or frozen like statues beneath a bush.

Jack was just beginning to loosen up and frisk about when he discovered a hole in the wire fence. I had overlooked it. He simply hopped through and continued to wander. He was really free now.

I followed at a discreet distance, filming from time to time, not wanting to lose contact any sooner than necessary. Occasionally, in response to my voice, he would hop to within ten feet of me. I shall always remember the experience of wandering through the desert that day, with Jack hopping nearby unafraid.

Suddenly he leaped into the air and streaked away. With graceful bounds of a freedom he had never known, he rapidly vanished. I shouldered my camera and, with a pang of regret at having seen the last of Jack, headed for the truck. I had gone only fifty feet when, like a streak of lightning, Jack cut across close in front of me, going in the opposite direction, and vanished again into the distance. Moments later I was again startled when he shot by in still another direction.

I shouted farewell after his retreating form and wished him luck. After all, he had four lucky rabbit's feet and had already lived longer than most rabbits. As for me, his brief stay with me had enriched my knowledge of one of the most often seen but least understood creatures of the desert.

5

SNOOPY

My first filming assignment had dealt with one of the most abundant but least known of desert creatures. In my second effort for the *Lassie* show I turned to one of the most common and most endearing of wild pets, the raccoon.

Probably no other animal has captured the love and admiration of the American people as has the raccoon. He is native only to the Americas and is found in almost every state. Extremely adaptable, he survives in deserts, mountains, and along both coasts. With his bandit-like face he is among the most photogenic of animals. His clever and dexterous hands enable him to pry into the most unexpected places. He adapts well to captivity, likes humans and is easy to care for.

The subject of my new project came to me as a small bundle of fur with half-opened eyes. I named him Snoopy, because, with his masked face, it seemed appropriate. Little did I know how well he was going to live up to his name.

Like Jack, Snoopy became a bottle addict. For the first few weeks he drank a mixture of milk and pablum from a bottle which had the nipple orifice enlarged to allow the thick mixture to pass through. Lying on his back, he would suck and slurp while I held the bottle. As he grew more coordinated with his feet he would actually hold the bottle himself. By the end of a feeding session there was an incredible mess over his face, hands, the floor, the walls or anything else he came into contact with.

I began filming as soon as he was able to use his small legs. There was never any worry about losing Snoopy. To the contrary, he was always six inches behind my heels. I had to get someone, usually my wife, Judi, to hold him while I moved off and set up the camera. Then, when I was ready, she released Snoopy and I got a fine shot of him coming toward the camera.

I had to devise various methods of outsmarting him in order to get a variety of shots. For instance, I would let him see me in a certain spot long enough for him to get a good fix on me. Then Judi would pick him up and shield him from me while I moved the camera to an entirely different position. As soon as he was returned to the ground his tiny legs headed him in the direction of my original position while I filmed from another. After running fifty feet he would usually pull up, look around bewildered, whimper, and take a few paces in another direction. It was fine footage of a little waif lost in the forest. When he had tried several directions and was beginning to get upset, I would call to him and get a good shot of him becoming reoriented. He would lose no time in racing to me and would climb up my leg to be cuddled in a joyful reunion.

His interest in the bottle persisted even after he began eating solid food. For him the bottle was a lazy way to guzzle his favorite beverage. Snoopy wasn't the only individual in our family who enjoyed the bottle.

Kristine, our youngest child, was only six months old at the time we got Snoopy. As Snoopy grew and became more mobile, he and Kristine became good friends. She thoroughly enjoyed feeling his soft hands as he explored the beads on her walker. Shrieks of joy from Kristine would accompany his gentle exploration of her hands and feet. He was especially good at untying her shoes and took great delight in making off with articles of clothing.

There was bound to be a confrontation between these two sooner or later, especially as there was a mutual attraction to certain objects such as rattles, beads and other toys. As long as Kristine willingly gave these up, which she often did, there was no problem. Of all her possessions, the one she prized was the one Snoopy wanted the most—her bottle. Since our idea of sanitation didn't include the mutual use of baby bottle by baby and raccoon, we had to take precautions. Nevertheless, eventually there was a slip-up.

Raccoons love to climb trees . . .

During one of Kristine's afternoon feedings Snoopy somehow gained entrance to the house. By now he was two-thirds grown and no more a toddler. The baby lying on the floor, happily guzzling her bottle, attracted his immediate attention. With no apologies whatsoever he rudely snatched the plastic bottle from her hands and proceeded to get busy on the nipple. Naturally the child was upset and let out a howl, which brought Judi running.

. . . or tripods!

Snoopy, sensing that what he had done wasn't exactly acceptable, headed for one of the bedrooms at full speed, bottle and all. There he took refuge beneath a bed and proceeded to extract every drop from the bottle, with much accompanying noise. From that day on, that was Snoopy's bottle, although we seldom filled it. It was his security blanket upon which he could always depend. It always remained under the bed, where he could find refuge when he got into trouble around the house.

Gradually he acquired a little hoard of playthings—a rattle, curlers, a rubber ball, and, in a stroke of luck, the baby's pacifier. All of these he secreted in various parts of the house to use when needed.

Most of his days were spent in his outdoor cage, but frequently he was allowed in the house. The length of time he was allowed inside was inversely proportional to the amount of damage he did. The more damage, the less time. By the time he was full grown he had pretty well developed his technique for enjoying the house.

To Snoopy, the house was Disneyland—a place to go to and have a good time with one thing in mind: time was limited. This seemed to be the dominating factor influencing his behavior when he was allowed in. He was a creature on borrowed time, out to make every second count.

By bribing him with delicacies such as grapes or marshmallows we could keep him somewhat under control. For a time anyway. Then his interest would turn to things other than food. After all, he could eat anytime.

The low kitchen cabinets were always good for some fun. Deftly he would open them and reach for the shiny pots and pans. Since Judi wasn't especially thrilled with the sight of raccoon handprints all over her cookware, we reserved one cabinet just for Snoopy. In it we put old pots and pans, silverware, and other delightful objects. He soon learned that this cabinet was his alone, and it became a favorite spot. However, even this spot was good only for a few minutes, and then he was off to other challenges.

As the evening wore on he would usually get more and more wound up. By nine o'clock his was a devil-may-care attitude, a philosophy of "Time's awasting, there's lots more to do." Chewing on an electric cord could always get a rise out of the humans. And then there was the challenge of seeing how high he could climb up the drapes before someone caught him. There was also the fireplace. If he was quick enough he could usually get a couple of cold black cinders out onto the carpet before we could even get out of our chairs.

With the vision of black footprints all over the house, the order would go out from my wife to "get him out of here!" It was then that Snoopy, ears laid back and fur bristling, would put into effect the evasive portion of his evening performance. The ultimate goal, of course, was one of his corners of refuge beneath the bed. From our tone of voice he knew he was in trouble and wasted no time in scooting out of sight. Moments later sucking sounds would emanate from within as he locked onto either his pacifier or an empty bottle. In due time I would be able to extract him by bribing him with a marshmallow. I'd deposit him outside in his cage and another evening would be over.

His quarters outside were not large but were adequate. About five feet square and six feet high, the chicken-wire enclosure boasted a small tree and a sleeping box. On the concrete floor was a wading pool which was always a mess. It seems that anything and everything a raccoon comes in touch with must be taken into water. Consequently, a daily flushing of his pool was necessary.

At first the cage was secure enough for the small raccoon. But as he grew and his dexterity increased I found it necessary to make week-by-week improvements. There were many times when I felt

Up to his armpits in an interesting hole.

Snoopy and Oliver the otter at play.

confident that he was confined, only to find, minutes later, that he was scratching at the back door. Over and over again I repaired the cage, and over and over again Snoopy figured a way to extricate himself. More than once I spent a cold night trying to fix his latest exit after being awakened at 2 A.M. by his scratching at our bedroom window.

Usually these self-exiting adventures went no farther than our back door. His great compelling drive, it seemed, was to get into the house. I suppose it was inevitable that Snoopy's unscheduled appearances at the door would cause a bit of a problem someday.

Judi had invited some new women acquaintances for an afternoon get-together. Not one to do anything halfway, she prepared diligently for her guests. Of course, making sure the house was spotless was of prime concern. When she heard a knock at the door some fifteen minutes before the guests were scheduled to arrive, everything was in order, the refreshments were set out, and she was finishing up a few last-minute things. She hurried to the door, opened it, and saw no one. An instant later her feet were nearly knocked from under her as a burly little body charged in: Snoopy.

In an absolute panic she tried to round him up. It was useless. Snoopy must have sensed the utter horror in Judi's voice, because he rose to his finest hour. With incredible accuracy he opened the kitchen cabinets while on a full run. On the second lap around he managed to strew pots and pans everywhere. Then he rounded the corner and headed down the hall, ears down and snorting like an old sow, with Judi in hot pursuit with a rolled newspaper.

My den was his favorite room. It was here that I spent hours playing with him when he was small. It was his home before he was moved to the outside cage. And also it was a refuge for him because here I would take him if things got too hot for him in the rest of the house and I didn't want to put him outside.

Daughter Kristine giving the bottle to a coatimundi baby, a member of the raccoon family.

So now, at a full gallop, he hurtled through the door and took refuge beneath my desk. There he made his defense. But Judi was through. He could have the den. Let Kent get him out when he came home. With that she slammed the door and staggered into the kitchen to clean the mess. Moments later the bell rang and she greeted the first of her guests.

One of Judi's greatest assets is that she can gather her wits about her in a crisis. With the appearance of her guests, she fully regained her composure and proceeded to carry off an almost perfect party. Eventually she lost herself in enjoying her friends, so much so that she didn't hear the occasional crashes from my den.

As the afternoon wore on, one of the women expressed an interest in seeing the rest of the house. Judi was ready. Every room was spotless. She had, by now, completely forgotten the incident with Snoopy.

Room by room the inspection party moved through the house, poking into each doorway. But the last door was closed. With complete innocence Judi opened the door wide and announced, "And this is Kent's den." Gasps of horror filled the air as all eyes stared at the scene.

It was an absolute shambles. From all appearances a massive earthquake had struck but somehow affected only this room. Nearly all the books had been flung from the bookcase and scattered across the floor. The contents of the wastebasket were littered about. The entire roll of toilet paper from the adjacent bathroom had been unrolled and wound about the room like a giant web spun by some equally giant but intoxicated spider. A mysterious white powder was liberally sprinkled over the floor, and almost every square inch of wall surface to a height of two feet was imprinted with white powdered handprints. The empty can of bowl cleanser lay in the center of the room.

In the bathroom black smears were everywhere. Footprints to the tub showed where countless plunges by dexterous hands had expertly extracted every bit of foreign matter from the drain. Now the black gooey stuff was smeared everywhere.

The medicine cabinet above the sink had been opened and the contents dumped into the basin and the toilet. The toothpaste tube had been salvaged and its contents squeezed out through countless tooth punctures. The empty tube now lay quietly at the bottom of the toilet bowl, along with miscellaneous objects ranging from tweezers to pill bottles.

From somewhere beneath the heap of toilet paper in the den there was a stir. Seconds later Snoopy stared back at the unbelieving eyes with as angelic a face as one could imagine. Who would ever believe that one creature could cause all that mess? Judi did. With a slam of the door she led the ladies from the room. Not in the wildest imagination could any of their houses ever top the mess Judi's guests had just seen.

Snoopy, relaxing after a hard day before the cameras.

Snoopy's film career continued for another year, and he appeared in various films. Since he was a fairly easy animal to handle, I was asked to take him to Canada, where a producer friend was making a Disney film. For a summer he lived on an island near Victoria while the crew filmed. At summer's end he was returned to me in fine shape.

Less than three months later, he was gone. While we were away for the weekend he made another one of his innumerable escapes from his cage. Since no one was home, he wandered away. There were rumors that this time he had escaped via a nearby orchard and that he lived a long life filching avocados and oranges from the local growers. But we never saw him again.

It wasn't easy to forget Snoopy. For months afterward we were frequently reminded of him—by a forgotten trinket stored by him behind the sofa, a pair of dirty handprints on the wall behind a table, the back door with its paint worn off by countless scratchings for admittance. And outside, at his cage, the chewed hole in the wire with bits of gray fur still clinging to the broken strands.

6

COPING WITH CLOWNS

In my role of photographer of the animal episodes for specific *Lassie* shows, I was constantly searching for unusual animal actors. The varieties of animals that could be used for the shows were limited. Snakes and rats were definitely out. The ideal subject was an animal that was appealing in both looks and action, one with which the children in the audience could empathize and which had no bad connotations that might be offensive to adults. The story had to have the element of danger to a helpless animal so that Lassie could be the heroine (actually the hero, since the role of this famous female collie was always played by a male dog). Baby animals such as Snoopy were always the best subjects. But in most species the babies appear only at one time of the year. I needed an adult subject.

I could hardly believe my luck when a friend told me he knew of a man who had two river otters he wanted someone to take for a year or more. Otters, from all that I had heard about their playful characteristics, should be ideal for my purpose. The two otters in question had been raised from pups by this man. They had had the run of the house until his recent marriage, but now they were confined to an outdoor cage. He was in the process of moving and, for the time being, had no place at his new home for the animals.

The man was agreeable to my filming the otters while I boarded them for him. He was quite concerned, however, that I build a proper

73

cage. A meeting at my home was arranged so that I could show him the enclosure I would provide.

I designed a cage about twenty feet long and six feet wide. A concrete slab with drain was imperative so that the cage could be hosed down easily. Since otters are water-loving animals, it was also necessary to build a pool in the cage. The pool I designed was about five by two feet and about two feet deep; it was small, but adequate for their water games. The four sides of the cage itself were of solid wood fencing about four feet high. Across the top I fastened heavy wire netting. It looked secure.

The man arrived one evening with his wife and examined the enclosure. He repeated several times that the rascals were escape artists, but he said he figured the cage would hold them. His wife seemed a bit eager that we should have the animals. In a moment of carelessness she muttered that she sure would be glad to get rid of them. I figured that meant she was anxious to get into her new home. My wife thinks she was trying to warn us. In any case, the time was set for me to pick up the otters.

It was evening when I reached the man's home, situated in an expensive area of the Hollywood Hills. I backed my van up to his garage and opened the van door. He unfolded an elaborate plan to get the animals into the vehicle. It was no easy task, he informed me, to get them from point A to point B. His wife nodded in agreement and told him to get on with it.

He stationed me at the van door with instructions to be quick with the door once they were in. He stationed his wife at the gate to the otters' pool, because, as he said, "If they get in there we'll be here all night." Then with one hand he grabbed some raw chicken necks and with the other he took hold of his black Labrador retriever. With the dog dragging behind reluctantly, he approached the otters' cage door some seventy-five feet away.

I watched in fascination to get the first glimpse of my new subjects. I didn't have long to wait. The lock was barely out of the hasp when the door burst open and two black bodies charged out. They looked like nothing I had ever seen before. Their movements were fluid and quick. Otters are the largest members of the weasel family and have a characteristic hump in their backs as they run.

These two were about three feet long including their heavy tails. Their heads were rather flat, and they had a perpetual quizzical expression.

They seemed to be interested in everything. At first they made a beeline for the swimming pool, but the wife effectively blocked their entrance. With courage born of strong motivations, she swatted them away with a newspaper. Then they saw the dog, who struggled desperately to get away from his owner's grasp.

Now the second phase went into action. As the man dragged the dog toward the van, the otters followed, nipping and nudging the poor creature. Soon they all stood at the rear bumper in a seething, writhing mass of bodies.

Then phase three. He showed the otters the chicken necks and tossed a handful into the van. Instantly both otters leaped into the van and I slammed the door.

"It worked!" he fairly shouted. His wife was beside herself with joy. Even the poor dog looked relieved. As I drove out of his driveway the man shouted one last instruction: "Don't let them loose around kids!"

A small seed of apprehension germinated as I turned down the street and out onto the freeway for the one-hour drive home. With every mile it grew, because I could hear terrible gnawing and chewing sounds coming from the rear of the van. I hoped it would hold together until we got home. Added to the scene was a powerful musky odor that nearly choked me, even with the windows rolled down. As members of the weasel family, otters possess glands which secrete an odoriferous musk when the animals are excited.

By the time I turned into my driveway, the sounds from the back had quieted somewhat. Probably either escaped or killed themselves, I thought grimly.

Just as the owner had laid elaborate plans to get the otters into the van, so I did to get them out. There were two ways from the van to the otters' cage in the back yard. One was around the side of the house, quite a circuitous route and pitch black at night. The other way was through the house. I chose to go through the house.

Quickly I briefed the family. The kids were to stay in their rooms behind closed doors until all was clear. The front and back doors were propped open. The otter cage door also was opened. Judi would follow along behind me, closing doors to prevent any escape. She looked apprehensive as I went out to open the van door.

Since I didn't have a black Labrador and I was sure the otters wouldn't be interested in chicken necks, the only thing I could do was grab. As the van door opened, a black body squeezed out. I uttered a prayer that it wouldn't bite too hard and scooped up the squirming otter in my arms.

My grip a bit uncertain, I raced for the front door of the house, hoping I could hang on until I reached the cage. With the black otter body weaving wildly in and out of my arms I entered the house. Judi gasped once but, according to plan, slammed each door behind me. In seconds I dumped the animal into the cage and closed the door.

Then with a jolt I remembered I hadn't closed the van door. Seconds later I peered into the van, expecting to see nothing. Instead, there was the apparently lifeless body of the female otter. The trip had left her exhausted, and I was able to pull her out and hurriedly deposit her in the cage. Then I sprinkled them both with cold water and returned to the house.

Several times that evening I checked on them. The female was recovering from her sickness, which apparently had been brought on by excitement and overheating. By the time we retired to bed both animals were swimming happily in their pool. "At least I have a pair of otters now. Whether I can ever film them remains to be seen," I told Judi.

It was Labor Day weekend, and the next morning was to be a lazy one. No work, no reason to get up early. So it was with some annoyance that I heard the telephone ring at 7 A.M.

The neighbors on our street are congenial people and not the sort to make trouble. Most of them are aware that I often have unusual pets in the back yard. If some strange animal turns up in the neighborhood, it's natural for them to call me rather than the police.

I answered the phone sleepily. It was the neighbor on our west side. Rita was a charming English girl who normally was very calm. This time, however, I detected a note of hysteria in her voice. "Please come quickly," she stammered. "Your thing is in our bedroom!"

It was impossible! My "things" were in their cage. Something told me I had better not even check the cage. Get next door as soon as possible!

Good neighbors cannot be fully appreciated until they have experienced a scene such as I saw in that bedroom and will still speak to you. It was absolute havoc. All members of the family were standing on chairs, dressers, or whatever, looking with horror at the bed. There was Oliver, the male otter, happily diving in and out of the covers, off the bed, under it, and back up on top. He was having a glorious time while the family watched, petrified.

With no attempt at apologies, I scooped the animal up and retreated as quickly as possible, looking at no one. It was terribly embarrassing. It's one thing to have an animal on the loose, but to have him invade someone's bedroom is another matter.

Outside I found Olive, the female, and somehow herded both back into the cage. After repairing the cage I went next door for formal apologies. What a horrifying experience to be awakened by an animal which you had never seen before in your life. Thank goodness for calm, rational people like the McIntoshes. I shudder to think what my own family would have done if it had happened to us instead. After that shattering initiation into the world of otter owners, I hoped beyond hope that things would be tame from there on.

Oliver and Olive were soon adjusted to their new home. It would be safe to say that they adjusted far more quickly than did their new owners. For the first few days I peered cautiously through the wire cage roof at these overgrown weasels. They seemed friendly enough now, especially Oliver. Standing tall on his hind legs, he chirped and appeared eager to make up for his bad behavior. Their bodies were so supple they seemed to be without a spine. In their bathing pool they went around and around, creating a miniature whirlpool which eventually sloshed most of the water out. An everyday ritual, on my part, was to refill the pool.

After a week of cautiously eyeballing them it seemed time to let them out into the back yard. Sooner or later I would have to take them out on location for filming, and the back yard was the first step in that direction.

I chose a time when the family was gone for the day. If the

animals were going to get out of control, I certainly didn't want an audience. After checking the gates to make sure the yard was secure, I opened the cage door.

Oliver peered out cautiously and uttered a few low quizzical grunts. Olive peered over his shoulder. Both acted as if it was some kind of trap. Finally they emerged and began to race full speed around and around the yard. They were exuberant and joyful at having so much freedom. Not until then had I realized just how fast they could run. The wet grass attracted them, and as they hit it at high speed they would flop on their bellies and slide along, uttering chirps of joy.

Truly here were nature's most fun-loving clowns. The otter is one of the few animals that possess a playful streak. Like two kids at a park, Olive and Oliver raced, wrestled and tumbled. They continued this play for a half hour, scarcely noticing that I was watching. Then Oliver approached me and rubbed his sleek body against my leg. I scratched his head and he rolled over for the same treatment on his belly. We were friends, at least for the present.

After an hour I decided to get them back into the cage. And herein the problem lay. No amount of coaxing or bribery would get them through that door. Nothing can be more elusive than a stubborn otter. Time and time again they paused in front of the open door and teased me before dashing off in the opposite direction.

Just when it seemed they had permanently taken over the yard, I stumbled upon a way. Figuring that since they loved water so much I could use it as a lure, I tried squirting water from the hose to coax them into the cage. To my amazement they were terrified of the stream of water. Incredible! Water-loving animals afraid of water? Apparently they loved water but only on their own terms. The jet from the hose sent them running, and in minutes I had them safely in the cage.

Now that I had the secret for controlling them in the back yard, I could let them out every day for a romp. Soon the time came when I let them loose with an audience. And it was then that Oliver exposed himself as a pest. As soon as he saw Judi and her friend Betty, he made a direct line for their feet. One sharp nip on the heel of each woman sent them screaming and clambering for the top of a convenient table. I hastened to obey their demands to "get those things back in their cage."

Oliver was a habitual nipper. His was not malicious biting, but merely a way of saying, "Let's play." It didn't matter to him if we didn't want to play. Consequently the practice didn't go over well with my friends and my wife. His bites weren't confined to just other people. Since I was finally the only one in the yard while they were loose, I became Oliver's target. It became a game with him to see if he could sneak up on me and deliver the goods. It was something I had to learn to live with.

During the next several months before I began filming, the otters showed their talents as escape artists. With their sharp teeth and powerful jaws they slowly chewed up their cage, and it became a daily ritual for me to survey the night's damages and make appropriate repairs each morning. In spite of my efforts there were times when their endeavors paid off.

On one particular morning I left early without checking the cage. About two hours later, at eight o'clock, I returned home. As soon as I turned down our street I knew something was wrong. In nearly every doorway stood a housewife, looking grimly down the street, her children peering out fearfully from behind. I didn't need to look far to see the problem.

Oliver and Olive, enjoying themselves immensely, were loping along the sidewalk, looking for someone or something to play with. Their strange looks intimidated everyone. Even the neighborhood dogs tucked their tails between their legs and retreated before them. Right behind the otters came my poor wife, newspaper in hand, trying valiantly to stop their progress. At the sight of me, Judi let it be known quite clearly what she thought about my otters.

There was only one way to head them off. Quickly I disconnected our hose and with it on my shoulder raced to get a lead on them. Once ahead of them, I stopped at the closest house and hooked up. Then as the otters loped toward me I blasted them with a powerful stream of water. They pulled up sharp and reversed direction. I had them on the run. I disconnected and hooked up at the next house for another blast. Now that the otters were retreating, a few brave dogs emerged to bark lustily. House by house the mothers and children stepped from their doorways to watch my progress. On down the street I went, hooking up and disconnecting as I went. It looked ridiculous, but it worked. Finally I headed the otters into our own yard and into their cage.

Now the mothers released their children to go to school. I doubt that the teachers believed the students' story of why they were late.

Little by little I was becoming acquainted with the characteristics of these two otters. Their misadventures, while somewhat nerve-shattering to me, did provide me with information on their behavior. Soon the day came when I selected a location for filming. It was about fifty miles north of us, along the Sespe Creek in the Los Padres Forest.

In order to control the wanderings of the animals, I had to construct an enclosure some two hundred feet in diameter. Made of chicken wire four feet high, this fence completely enclosed a portion of the creek, including a deep pool. It took several days for me to set it up. It had to be buried a foot in the ground and carefully camouflaged behind shrubs and trees.

Once the location was prepared I had only to get the otters up there. Remembering the ordeal of their first car ride, I didn't relish the trip. But since it had been almost six months since that ride, it was fairly easy to coax them into the van.

For the week's filming I had hired a young fellow who had worked for me before, and after loading the otters I stopped by his place and picked him up. As we headed up the mountains the gnawing and chewing sounds began from the rear of the van. For several miles Roger and I chatted and I told him of these delightful animals we were going to work with. With each mile the sounds grew louder and the odor became unbearable. Roger began to cast nervous glances toward the rear and seemed to lose the enthusiasm that he had had earlier.

By the time we arrived at the location the sounds had ended as before. Before releasing the animals I set up the camera and prepared for filming. Their escape might be the only footage I would ever get, I thought grimly. Roger opened the door with great apprehension.

On location with Oliver and Olive.

Oliver leaped out and headed for the water. Once again, however, Olive was sick. I carried her to a cool spot and laid her down.

At the stream Oliver dived in and joyously streaked from one end of the pool to the other. After several times he came out on the sand to roll and dry himself. Minutes later he returned to the pool. All that day I filmed Oliver as he played and swam in the water. Toward evening Olive roused and joined him.

I was worried that they would escape from the enclosure during the night. But, having been raised in captivity, they had completely reversed the normal otter pattern of nocturnal activity and daytime sleeping, and they promptly went to sleep beneath a tree at nightfall.

The great fears that I had of losing them were unfounded. The attraction of the large natural pool kept them from wandering. I did find it necessary, however, to wear full clothes even when in the water, due to Oliver's nasty habit of biting. Even so, my legs and arms were soon a mass of dark-blue bruises.

This affinity Oliver had for the human body became my biggest problem. I could put up with the biting if it were not for the fact that it was interfering with filming. In order to deliver his "friendly" gestures, Oliver had to hover around me constantly. With him so close at hand it was impossible to record any underwater footage of the otters' graceful swimming.

Finally I had to change my methods. The underwater shots would have to be done when Oliver was taking a nap. I would then film Olive in the water. She was more timid and would be easier to film. This usually worked for several minutes until Oliver awoke and realized he was missing out on the action. Once he entered the water I would stop filming and leave. No use enduring any more of Oliver's love bites than necessary.

Finally there came a time when I was getting such good footage of Olive that I couldn't stop when Roger called that Oliver had entered the pool. I was floating on my stomach just beneath the surface, engrossed in keeping the camera on Olive as she performed watery acrobatics, when I felt Oliver nudge my shoe with his nose. Then I felt him bump me again farther up my leg, and then at my waist. Then for a moment he seemed to leave. All of a sudden there was a sharp pain as he clamped down hard on my right ear. Needless to say, I reacted loudly and hurried toward shore, while Oliver orbited about me, chirping gleefully.

At the end of that week I had successfully filmed all the necessary scenes for my portion of the upcoming *Lassie* show. I had gotten far better footage than I had expected and had had remarkably little trouble controlling the otters. Nevertheless, it was with a good deal of relief that I returned Olive and Oliver to the safety of the home cage.

Some weeks later while at the studio I learned to my horror that the producer wanted me to bring the otters to the Malibu Mountains to be filmed on location with Lassie and the rest of the cast. Try as I did, I could not talk him out of the idea. Visions of my otters disrupting an entire camera crew of fifty people flashed through my mind. But the producer was insistent. I reluctantly agreed, on one condition—that a sturdy cage be constructed at the location, to house the animals until they were needed. He assured me it would be done. With some misgivings I agreed on a date.

The location was at the edge of a small private natural lake in a beautiful mountain setting. True to his word, the producer had had his crew construct a cage. I took one look and told him it would never hold them. He looked at me incredulously and said that the crew had put wolves in it before and they hadn't escaped. I examined the cage closer and had them make a few changes. It still looked flimsy, but I had to give it a try. The otters were destroying my van while we waited.

We had no more than closed the door on the cage when someone shouted, "There they go!" Sure enough, both animals were galloping toward the lake. I knew if they reached the lake we could forget any filming. I headed for Oliver, because I knew I could pick him up. I told the others to grab Olive. I didn't tell them that she bit like a tiger when picked up. I managed to get Oliver and hustled him back to the cage. Olive made it into the lake and vanished.

I stationed Roger at the cage to make sure Oliver didn't get out again. Oliver was so angry that when someone passed within ten feet he would growl and bite a large hole in the wire side, and Roger would have to wire it closed. All the members of the crew had to come by and see Oliver perform this feat. I heard some of them say that they sure were glad they hadn't been able to grab Olive. Secretly, so was I.

About midmorning Lassie's trainer arrived with the canine star. He had been informed that he was to work his dog with an otter, so he had come by to see the animal. He was yet ten feet away when Oliver lunged at the wire and bit a large hole in it. That was it. "Not with my dog you don't!" the trainer bellowed to the producer. Hastily they rewrote the script to avoid any contact between Lassie and Oliver.

Later in the day a scene was set up that I thought we could do with Oliver. The setting was an old cabin, which was supposed to be the home of an old-timer who loved otters. In the story Oliver's mate is in trouble and he comes to the old man for help. For this particular scene the producer wanted the otter to run along a trail and come to the cabin.

Tied in front of the cabin, contentedly chewing her cud, was the old man's cow, Clementine. The director asked me what I thought Oliver would do when he saw the cow. I figured he'd bite the cow just as he did everything else. On hearing this, the owner of the cow exploded, but the director smoothed it over as only a joke. But I wasn't joking. At any rate, the director hoped Oliver would greet the cow in some way. I told him Oliver probably would.

The scene was set up. Fences were built to control Oliver. The cameras were ready. The cow was chewing her cud. The director wanted to follow his usual practice and rehearse the scene several times before filming. I quietly informed him that he would have only one chance and no more. He had better film the first time, because there wouldn't be a second. He agreed.

Oliver was taken down the trail out of camera sight and held in a small cage. On cue we released him, and I called him. He performed like a veteran, loping down the trail exactly as ordered. I could hear the director muttering, "Beautiful, beautiful." At the sight of Clementine, Oliver pulled up sharply. Never before had he seen an animal as large as a cow. Its very size intrigued him immensely.

In fascination he ambled over to Clementine, who, by now, had stopped chewing her cud and was staring a bit nervously. Closer he moved until he was directly in front of the cow. Then, standing as tall as he could, he looked the cow squarely in the face. At this point Clementine bent down to sniff this strange creature. Oliver seized the opportunity. With a quick move he clamped onto the nose of the cow and gave it all he had. The cow fairly exploded and bolted into the brush, the director yelled, "Cut!" and the cow trainer leaped the fence to retrieve his animal. Blood was streaming down her well-groomed neck, and the owner was understandably upset.

"She's the only trained cow in Hollywood," he moaned, "and now she's so nervous she'll probably forget everything I've taught her."

Oliver, meanwhile, had ambled over to a water bucket and was busy playing as if nothing had happened. The director was happy with the scene. "We can cut it just before the otter bit the cow!" he exclaimed gleefully.

That concluded the studio work with the otters. After the crew left I set out to retrieve Olive. For the next three days I paddled around the lake in a rubber raft, trying to catch her. She was as elusive as the Loch Ness monster. A shiny head among the reeds on the far side of the lake would be my only clue. By the time I paddled over, she would be on the side I had started from. Fortunately for me, she wasn't able to catch her own food, and little by little I was able to coax her to a trap I had built on the shore. Several times I nearly had her, but she drew back and returned to the lake. Finally, when I thought I'd never get her, I was successful. Taking my otters home, I vowed never again to take them on location with a large crew.

The footage that I had shot was edited in with studio footage. When the show was completed the producer was very happy and felt that it was one of their best animal shows. As a fitting climax to my experience with otters, I was deprived of ever seeing the show. Returning from a filming trip on the day it was to be telecast, I had car trouble and arrived home a half hour too late. I never did see the results of my efforts.

Three months later the otters' owner called to say he was ready to have his animals returned. Though I wouldn't have believed it earlier, it was with mixed emotions that I delivered Olive and Oliver to him. They had been problems at times, but they had given me a rare close glimpse of the ways of a fascinating creature.

It is sad to realize that this animal which was once so numerous in our country's waterways is now seldom seen. Unfortunately for otters, their fur is valuable and they have been trapped commercially for decades. In most areas they are now protected, but it is the rare and lucky person who ever sees a river otter in its natural habitat.

7

A PRAIRIE-DOG
VILLAGE COMES
TO VISIT

In the interest of better relations with the neighborhood, I decided that my next subjects would be easier to work with than Olive and Oliver. Recollections of a trip to Wyoming on which I had watched a colony of prairie dogs had given me an idea for another show.

Prairie dogs belong to the squirrel family and get their name from their peculiar barking sound. At one time their villages covered thousands of square miles of the American West, and the little animals lived in harmony with the antelope, the bison and the Indian. But the arrival of the white man and his cattle spelled the end of the large prairie-dog villages. The ranchers looked upon the little rodent as a pest, a competitor for the range grass on which they grazed their cattle. In typical white-man fashion, they set out to exterminate the millions of prairie dogs. Today there remain only a few scattered colonies, where the remnants of a once thriving race live out their lives under the close surveillance of wildlife authorities.

The prairie dog is an attractive, energetic, likable creature. In him I saw a character which would work well in a *Lassie* show. I was fortunate enough to obtain four of these animals from a nearby zoo on a temporary basis, for filming. (It is unlawful for private individuals to keep prairie dogs in California.)

In nature the prairie dog is an amazing engineer capable of

building a network of underground burrows more intricate than installations of the Army Corps of Engineers. Their networks of tunnels were greatly responsible for allowing water to penetrate the hardpan of the Southwest. In this way the subterranean water reservoirs were replenished each rainy season. Much of the prairie dog's life is spent in his underground home. I wanted to be able to film the animals in such a subterranean dwelling, but to do this it was necessary to construct a set—an artificial burrow—that would afford the camera an underground point of view.

Inexpert at set building, and unaware that there were lightweight materials available, I toiled for a week in my back yard with wire mesh and mortar, making a covered structure four feet high, eight feet long and one foot wide, with one side of glass. Through this side I would be able to film the interior, which was supposed to simulate a cross section of a burrow and which had an opening to the roof so that the animals could go "above ground" when they wanted to.

I had an eager and sometimes helpful audience of neighborhood kids. I was already some kind of hero to them, since my back yard always had an odd assortment of exotic creatures. Now a virtual parade of children filed in and out of the yard, asking a thousand questions as to exactly what I was doing. I declined to admit to them that I wasn't sure exactly what I was doing.

By the time I had finished the set, it must have weighed a quarter ton. It took four men to put it in an upright position on blocks. And to this day it stands in the same spot. A monument to prairie dogs, I suppose.

Atop the structure I built a wire enclosure to contain the animals when they came up out of the burrow. The glass wall of the "underground" section was covered with a sheet of plywood when I wasn't filming, to give them privacy below.

The day came when I introduced the prairie dogs to their concrete home. They immediately plunged below to investigate the accommodations. It didn't take them long to realize that they couldn't alter the hard concrete burrow. But, like it or not, it was home. I provided dry grass, which they promptly hauled below; in minutes they had a comfortable nest. All in all, it was a good substitute for the real thing. After a few weeks I began filming them through the glass wall. They soon became adjusted to the sudden glare of light into their privacy.

Of course, the outdoor filming was to be the main part of the episode. For this I had to select a natural location that would resemble prairie-type country. After thorough searching I discovered, about an hour's drive from my house, a meadow that simulated very closely the natural habitat of prairie dogs. I obtained permission from the property owner and set to work.

I first had to enclose a large area with a two-foot-high chicken-wire fence. Just as with the otters, these prairie dogs had to be confined within a certain area; otherwise I would be constantly trying to round them up. The enclosed area was selected to take the best advantage of the scenic background. Camera angles had to be care-

Prairie dogs at Kent's handmade hole.

fully planned in order to make full use of the limited filming area.

I also had to create my own prairie-dog village. Although my prairie dogs were well equipped for digging, I had absolutely no way of controlling their choice of where they would dig, and no way of limiting the depth of their holes. It became obvious that I would have to do the digging for them before introducing them to the location.

Once again I had to plan carefully. Since I was trying to create the illusion of a prairie-dog village and had only four animals, I had to make up for the deficiency in prairie dogs by digging numerous holes. If, in the film, the viewer saw dozens of holes, only four of which were occupied, his imagination would tell him the other animals were in their burrows at the moment.

For two days I busied myself digging the holes in the appropriate spots. One of the interesting features of a prairie-dog burrow is that the animals cleverly build a dike around each occupied hole to prevent water from running into the hole during storms. Consequently I had to build each hole with a dike. The holes were only fifteen inches deep and had wire bottoms to prevent the animals from

Filming an adult burrowing owl, an underground dweller.

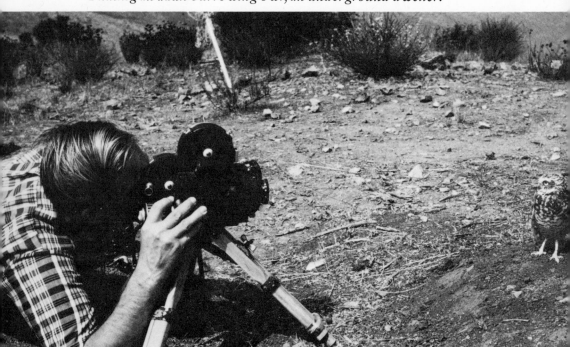

deepening the burrows. The dikes had to be built up with mud, packed hard to hold shape and then covered with dry sand.

On the second day of this time-consuming job I noticed a ranch pickup truck stopping on the highway a quarter mile away. I paused briefly on my hands and knees to look and then resumed my work. The pickup left, but returned an hour later. I could see the ranch hands looking with great interest in my direction.

I was in the midst of mixing up a fine batch of mud when they drove up. For several minutes they just stared while I patted the muddy mixture around the hole. Then one of them broke the silence and asked the inevitable question: "Just what are you doing, anyway?"

Without pausing in my work, I grinned up at them and said, "Building prairie-dog holes,"

There were blank looks, and one of the men said, "Oh."

Another long silence while I continued to work. Then: "But there ain't any prairie dogs in this entire state."

"There will be when I get the holes dug," I answered. Without another question they drove off, no doubt wondering about my sanity.

With the holes dug and the dikes built, I was ready to introduce my stars to their temporary home. I was greatly satisfied with my efforts. The holes looked genuine to me. The prairie dogs too seemed to recognize the holes. No sooner had they been released than they raced to the top of the burrow mounds just as if they themselves had built them. One of them dived down the hole, only to hit bottom in less than two feet. Hurriedly he exited and ran to another hole. Soon all of them were running from hole to hole, checking to see if any was genuine. Within seconds the fraud was exposed.

As if by mutual agreement, they all began to work on remodeling one burrow. For one thing, the dike was too high. One of them began digging furiously, while two others worked on the wire bottom. Moments later the wire was dislodged and the two below began to burrow down. The fourth prairie dog stood at the entrance, kicking sand out away from the hole. Such teamwork! It took them only a few minutes to double the hole depth, and while I watched in amazement all four prairie dogs vanished below the surface. Scrap-

Desert kitfox pauses before the camera.

ing sounds from below ground were the only indication that there were prairie dogs there.

Suddenly I realized that I was losing them and hadn't shot a foot of film. Grabbing a five-gallon jug, I poured water down the hole. Seconds later four sputtering, muddy prairie dogs exited from the hole in a hurry. From then on I had to be cautious and not let them get started on a hole.

They were easy animals to work with. Friendly creatures, they would often take tidbits from my hand or lie down in the shade of the camera for a rest. Once they knew the limits of their enclosure, they seemed to be satisfied. It was certainly better than the cage at home.

It was about the second week of filming when I again noticed the ranch pickup on the highway. Sure enough, it turned off for another investigation. This time I was busy filming when it approached. My four prairie dogs were cavorting about happily. The men watched the scene in silence. They asked no questions. I volunteered no answers. As they drove away I'm certain they must have thought, "Sure enough, them holes got prairie dogs in 'em now!"

As in most of the *Lassie* films I did, the animals had to get into a predicament so that Lassie could come to the rescue. In this episode the danger was twofold. A marauding badger, the natural enemy of prairie dogs, invades the colony and begins to dig up the holes, destroying the protective dikes in the process. In the midst of his sinister work he is frightened away by a flash flood which roars down out of the hills. Without the protective dikes, the holes rapidly fill with water, trapping the unfortunate animals below. In the nick of time Lassie arrives and unplugs an escape burrow for the prairie dogs.

With my part of the shooting over, I sent the film to the studios. The director went over the script and requested that I bring the animals to location for tie-in scenes with Lassie. Knowing how easy the prairie dogs were to work with, I happily agreed. Here perhaps was a chance to redeem myself for the disaster with the otters.

The special-effects people of the studio get some strange requests from directors, I am sure. But they were completely baffled when they received a request to build a prairie-dog village on the "back forty" of the studio lot. None of them had ever seen a prairie-dog village, much less built one. A desperate call was made to me by the special-effects foreman. There was no way to describe to him on the phone the way to build the village. I had to spend an afternoon with them. For four hours these highly paid technicians groveled in the dirt, mixed mud and learned the fine art of prairie-dog-hole construction. I seriously doubt that they have ever had another call for that special skill.

On the day of shooting I arrived on location in high spirits. I was prepared. My best animal was ready and I had a small net with me for emergencies. The net had always worked easily when I used it to catch the prairie dogs.

The scene required was a simple one. The director just wanted one prairie dog standing by his burrow while Lassie approached slowly and greeted him. It would be a good tie-in shot. I saw no reason it couldn't be done. On my locations I had used a collie as a double for Lassie in some scenes, and the prairie dogs had been very friendly. "It will be a snap," I told the director. While I waited for them to call me, I calmly consumed doughnuts and hot drinks from the studio caterer.

The call for prairie dogs finally went out. I was on! Taking my animal in a small cage, I walked over to the location. The director had placed an X on the exact spot.

"Put him there," he ordered.

I tried not to notice my little actor looking a bit wild-eyed at the forty-some people who milled around the set. Taking an empty plastic bucket, I placed it over the X. Then I raised it slightly and slipped my prairie dog beneath. This, I explained to the director, would keep him in position and calm until the exact moment of filming.

The trainer brought Lassie, but not before asking me quite gruffly if the prairie dog would bite. I reminded him that these were not otters. They were gentle animals and were scarcely a foot long. There was no need to worry.

With Lassie in position less than three feet away, I slowly lifted the bucket. The prairie dog took one look around him at all the people and took off like a shot—in and out of people's legs, over and under cables and tripods. Finally he took refuge beneath a sound truck. I hastily apologized, saying he was a bit shy because of all the people. Grabbing my net, I hurried to retrieve my reluctant actor. It was incredible how he instantly became an expert at dodging my net. Around and around I went, swinging wildly and always seeming to miss. Finally, in a stroke of luck, I cornered him against a reflector and scooped him up.

The procedure was repeated, with almost the same results. It

94

Undernourished, poor thing!

was getting embarrassing, so I suggested that we put a monofilament line on the prairie dog. I held him while a technician fastened the fine line around his neck and hooked it to an eyelet in the ground. Now he couldn't run away. But I had no more than replaced him when he chewed the line and was off again.

We repeated this again, using fine wire, but he twisted so violently that the wire broke. By this time the prairie dog was getting quite upset and so was everyone else. The director reminded me, not so gently, that it was costing the studio a hundred and fifty dollars for every ten minutes we wasted.

Then the special-effects man presented his next idea: a piece of thick black wire that looked ridiculously strong for the tiny animal. He told me with assurance that this was the same stuff he used to hold wolves in place.

The director now looked pleased. "That should hold the little rascal," he said.

On went the bucket. Lassie was put in position, the bucket was removed, and off streaked the prairie dog.

"What's going on?" thundered the director. "We can hold wildcats and wolves, but we can't hold that measly little rodent!"

From somewhere in the crew a piece of fine cable was passed to the special-effects man. He accepted it gratefully, for he was desperate now. In moments it was in place and the squirming prairie dog was put down. This time, no matter how the animal twisted, the wire held. Finally realizing he couldn't escape, he stood defiantly atop the burrow.

The cameras rolled and Lassie approached the prairie dog. "Closer," the director instructed, and the dog came nearer. Now they were almost muzzle to muzzle. The director was elated. Then the impossible happened. Having had just about all he could take, the prairie dog leaped with all fours upon Lassie's muzzle and began biting like a lunatic.

There was a gasp from the onlookers and a volley of swear words from Lassie's trainer. My first impulse was to pull the animal off Lassie's nose, but the trainer was afraid it might tear the dog's skin. Through it all, poor Lassie moved not a muscle. He and the prairie dog were practically eyeball to eyeball. At the slightest movement from anyone in the group the prairie dog would deliver another series of bites to Lassie's nose. I told everyone to be still, we would have to wait for the prairie dog to get off in his own sweet time.

For what seemed like an eternity, the prairie dog hung determinedly on; then, abruptly, he dropped off. Lassie was rushed to a first-aid station to determine what damage had been done. I scooped up my unpredictable animal and retreated to the car.

It was another embarrassing experience which proved once again that it is difficult to work with animals around a large crew. Lassie wasn't disfigured, but he certainly was disillusioned about the gentleness of small animals. His trainer had taken great care to see that no small animal ever harmed the dog. Now, he told me, he would have to begin training all over.

The show was completed and was a great success. The prairie-dog village looked authentic, and the underground shots were unique. I kept the animals for several more months because they were such interesting creatures. Ultimately, however, I had to return them to the zoo, where they were placed in spacious quarters with plenty of real earth to dig in.

In my brief acquaintance with these likable animals, I had learned much from observing their personalities and interrelationships. Each was different, but each had its place in the social order which, with a membership of only four, was a replica of the social structure that existed in the huge villages of earlier years.

It is regrettable that man's progress must spell doom to so many species. Fortunately, a few scattered colonies of prairie dogs are being preserved so that future generations can see this interesting animal living in its natural habitat.

8

ALL KINDS OF CATS

Since most of the wild creatures that dwell around us are nocturnal, they are seldom seen by the average person. There are species of animals so shy and secretive that only a trained zoologist can find evidence of their presence. One such animal is the ringtailed cat.

This delicate animal is about the size of a house cat but is not related to the cats. It is a member of the raccoon family and is distinguished by distinct rings on its bushy tail, as is the raccoon.

The ringtailed cat was a well-known nocturnal visitor to the cabins and shacks of early settlers of the West. So proficient was it in catching mice that it was welcomed and nicknamed the "miner's cat." But as suburbia crept across the continent, the ringtails retreated to the dark and quiet corners of the country. Today they are still abundant, but they seldom venture into the public eye.

My first encounter with a ringtail was but a moment in the blackness of night. While driving over a twisting mountain road, I came upon a confused ringtail trapped briefly in a highway tunnel. There was no traffic, so I stopped to watch the bewildered animal race from side to side, jumping at the granite walls. I was struck by the lithe beauty and grace of the small creature. Its delicate features and soft gray color were very appealing. When it stopped for a moment in the glare of the headlights, I saw its large brown eyes and inquisitive nose. Its gentle features were not at all in keeping with its role as a predator. For a moment it looked up at me, and then it streaked for the open end of the tunnel with its beautiful tail flowing smoothly behind. As it disappeared into the night I realized that here was an intriguing animal which would lend itself well to a *Lassie* film.

The search for a ringtail cat began. I didn't want to capture a wild animal; I hoped to find someone who had a tamed ringtail. Eventually I was lucky enough to locate, in a nearby town, a man who had had a pet ringtail for two years. I made an appointment with him and went to investigate. He had said on the phone that the animal was very gentle and a beautiful specimen, and she was. She peered out of her box and daintily accepted a tidbit from his hand. Although ringtails are predators and feed mainly on rodents, they do relish certain kinds of fruit. Apricots and peaches were this one's favorites. After having her snack she cleaned her face fastidiously and retreated to her sleeping box. An agreement was made and I returned home with the subject for my next film.

For a location I selected a forest area which is a known habitat of ringtails. In fact, it was only a few miles from the tunnel in which I had seen my first ringtail.

As in previous filming situations, I constructed a large enclosure, but I soon found that I didn't need it with the tame ringtail. She was a delightful animal to work with and was easily coaxed into various scenes. I was able to get all of the necessary close-ups, taking full advantage of the ringtail's attractive face and soft features.

In this *Lassie* episode the menace was to be provided by a marauding bobcat intent upon attacking the smaller ringtail (who, of course, would eventually be rescued by Lassie). A prerequisite was to have a bobcat. Once again I began the search for someone who had a workable animal.

In the Hollywood area there are a number of animal agencies that specialize in renting out animals for film-studio use. Most of them, I discovered, had bobcats. But I also discovered that their fees were geared to the big-studio budget. Definitely out of my category. I would have to look elsewhere.

Animal handlers and trainers are a special breed. While they all have a special attraction for animals, some are definitely more adept at exercising their special talent in a businesslike manner than others.

On location with the ringtailed cat.   (AL SEYLE)

I soon discovered that the poorer a trainer's business was, the cheaper were his fees. I began a systematic elimination of animal handlers, working my way down the scale until I found a fee that I could afford.

Just when I was about to settle a deal with one trainer for what I thought was a workable fee, I got wind of another trainer who, I had been told, was so desperate that he had taken on a job of cleaning cages for one of his competitors. This sounded like just the man I needed. I ceased all negotiations and set out to find him.

He proved as difficult to track down as a mountain lion. Several addresses I was given took me to vacant houses in remote canyons. There would be evidences of recent occupation, and nearby residents always confirmed that the man with the cats had lived there for a while, but he would be gone. I wasn't the only one looking for him, I learned. Various bill collectors were also on the trail. The more I discovered about him, the more convinced I became that here was a man I could deal with.

By asking countless questions and following endless leads, I finally came upon the right trail. At the end of a lonely canyon in dry, desolate country I found a dilapidated shack which at first glance appeared vacant like all the rest, but which upon closer investigation showed signs of current occupancy. An old beat-up station wagon was parked behind a weathered barn, evidently in an attempt to conceal it. As I walked toward the house I detected the unmistakable odor of dead flesh. On the ground were scraps of chicken parts and numerous chicken feathers were blowing about in the hot breeze.

I knocked at the door and waited in silence. I thought I detected a slight movement inside, but there was no answer. Again I knocked. Finally, after several minutes, the door opened and a voice said, "Yes?"

I peered through the rusty screen in an effort to see the source of the voice. It was nearly impossible. Vaguely I could make out the heavy form of the man.

"I understand you have some trained cats," I said.

"Who told you that?" he questioned cautiously. It was almost as if he was trying to keep it a secret. I could see why he wasn't doing too well.

My eyes were getting accustomed to the darkness behind the

door now. I thought I saw an occasional shadowy figure drift silently by. "Your name was given to me by another animal handler," I said. And then, in an attempt to break the ice, "I'm a film producer and I need to rent a bobcat."

Instantly the door opened and he emerged, thrusting out a puffy hand liberally decorated with scratches. "Yeah, I'm a trainer. Got some fine cats, too," he said.

He began an immediate rundown of the shows his animals had been in. It was an impressive list and I noted with silent amusement that his credits were almost exactly the same as those of the other trainers I had talked with. Strange how all trainers can claim the same credits, I thought.

The more he tried to impress me, the more I knew I could deal with him. Finally I asked if I could see his animals. He motioned for me to follow him into the house.

It was dark and musty-smelling inside. As my eyes adjusted to the darkness I saw an incredible sight. Here was a man who truly loved his animals—so much so that he lived with them, not they with him. In that one room there were half a dozen bobcats in various stages of relaxation. I had come to the right place, all right. All he had were bobcats.

In solemn tones he began to tell me about them. The cat on the bookshelf was an old female he had salvaged from the animal pound only an hour before it was to be executed. The one on the sofa was a reject from a competitor. The one on the kitchen table was the daughter of the one on the bookshelf. And she was mated to the one under the coffee table. And on it went.

He led me carefully across the room, stepping cautiously over chicken heads and cat feces. The cat on the bookshelf snarled nastily as we passed. The man opened a door and pointed inside. On the bed another cat was lying asleep. A red stain on the blanket looked fresh.

"That's Tammy," he said proudly. "Gave birth to two kittens last night right on my bed." Then a bit dejectedly, "But she ate 'em both before daylight."

Back outside I described to him the kind of scenes I needed. They weren't difficult, but they would require a certain amount of control over the animals. I expressed some doubt that his cats were

Bobcat.

capable of being kept under control. He retorted, with fur bristling, that there were none finer, and again related his list of credits.

His first price, as I expected, was exactly the price of the big outfits. Within ten minutes it was half, and in fifteen we had a deal that I could handle. We made arrangements to meet at my location the next Monday.

In anticipation of needing an extra helper, I had recruited Judi for the day. She had happily agreed to do what she could, and, considering the price, I figured it was a good deal. It would be an easy day's work, I told her.

When we arrived with the ringtail at the appointed place, the cat trainer was waiting, with two of his best animals in the back of his station wagon. He seemed a little surprised that my helper was Judi. I gathered from bits of conversation with him that he had once been married, but that his animals had gotten between him and his wife. I could see how that could easily happen with him.

We began with the simpler shots, those of the bobcat stalking through the forest in quest of prey. His cats did work well, and I was pleased with the footage. As we worked, however, the animals got warm in the sun and became cantankerous. Frequent rest periods were necessary for both animal and trainer. While the cat rested, the trainer patched up the newest scratches on his arms and hands.

The climax in the story, the bobcat's imminent attack against the helpless ringtail, was also the most critical part of the filming. I set up the scene as if the ringtail had taken refuge beneath a log and was cornered by the bobcat. By careful manipulation of the bobcat, we could bring them into close contact without endangering the ringtail.

With the ringtail in position, I set a reflector to bounce light onto her and instructed Judi to hold it firmly. Then the trainer brought the bobcat into the scene. The action I desired was one of the ringtail snarling defensively at the larger bobcat. But over and over again the ringtail just looked at the bobcat. No snarl or defensiveness whatsoever. It was as if the ringtail knew it was all make-believe. Even the bobcat seemed uninterested. Over and over again we tried. The sun was hot and the flies were at their best. Since I had stressed the importance of the scene, Judi stood unmoving with the reflector right on target.

Finally, after what seemed like hours, some activity started. The ringtail was losing patience at last with this ridiculous situation and was beginning to show a little spunk. I began to roll the camera. As I filmed, I noticed that the reflector was beginning to waver off target. Without looking up I cautioned Judi to hold it in position. A moment later the light left completely and there was a heavy thud as she collapsed in a heap beside the log. Passed out completely. It wasn't anything new to me, since she has always been one to pass out easily. I suppose that over the years I had grown to accept this phenomenon rather coolly. At any rate, the action was just starting and I couldn't stop filming for anything.

While the cat trainer looked on incredulously, I propped the reflector up with a stick, grabbed Judi under the arms, dragged her over into the shade, and then resumed filming the animals. The ringtail was performing marvelously, as was the bobcat, and in min-

Chipmunks are always available for "fill-in" shots.

utes I had the complete sequence. Not a word had been spoken about my poor wife, who now lay quiet and white beneath a pine. As I stopped filming, the trainer gestured toward her and wondered aloud whether she was all right. I replied that she'd do anything to get out of work. Moments later her eyelids flickered and she awoke. As soon as she felt better she sat up and we all had a good laugh. I'm sure that to this day that cat man remembers the photographer who was so dedicated to his camera that even his wife's fainting couldn't interfere.

There was always a variety of creatures housed in my back yard, and not all of them were used in films. Word would travel, and frequently someone would bring an animal or bird that he had found and couldn't care for.

Many times, these animals would be victims of progress, such as the three great horned owls who one spring were found in a tree which had been cut to clear land for a building. Sometimes they would simply be victims of man's inhumanity to his wildlife neighbors. Such was the case with an adult great horned owl that was brought to me with a mangled foot. Someone had placed a steel-jawed trap atop a fencepost, and when the owl landed during the night the trap snapped shut on its leg. The leg was nearly severed and gangrene had set in, so we had to destroy the beautiful creature.

Each year countless creatures meet death as the victims of irresponsible people with guns. Some die quickly, but others suffer a slow death. Often the people who are responsible are misinformed and ignorant of the real good these creatures may do.

Whenever one takes a wild animal as a pet one immediately deprives that animal of much of its natural instinct for survival. Sometimes it is possible to rehabilitate such animals so that they can be returned to the wild. More often, though, they accidentally get loose and may have a difficult time surviving. And there are times, too, when such an animal is mistaken for a wild, attacking beast and is destroyed.

Birdie Boy was an Idaho cougar who was captured when just a tiny kitten. A professional cougar hunter shot his mother and then traced her steps to a hollow log, where three kittens were found. A friend of mine obtained one of the kittens and proudly nursed him on a bottle for several weeks. The kitten was raised with love and kindness and grew to respond to humans with trust and affection.

Birdie Boy got his unusual name because of the birdlike call that young cougars have. Since his benefactor lived in the city, where it was illegal to have lions, his presence had to be kept a secret. However, as he grew and his vocalization began to be heard by the neighbors, questions were asked. When told that the strange sounds were only from Birdie Boy, no one questioned further. Everyone just assumed that the calls came from some kind of exotic pet bird. The secret was never discovered.

The young cat grew rapidly into a handsome cougar. As an energetic juvenile he was taken on long hikes in the hills, which he enjoyed thoroughly. He loved people and would flop on his side and purr loudly while his belly was scratched.

I met Birdie when he was about a year old. He was a beautiful cat with a thick, tawny coat. I used him for a few days while filming another *Lassie* show. We took the cougar into a spectacular mountain setting and proceeded to film. Basically all I needed were moving shots—running , stalking, peering down cliffs, etc. Most of them were easy to get.

The only problem was that Birdie never wanted to get too far from a human. In order to get good shots of him alone, we had to hide from him. This, of course, soon became a game which he played to the fullest. While his owner led him to the proper position, I readied my camera at another. His owner would wait until Birdie was preoccupied and then sneak away. In a short time the search would begin, and I would get wonderful footage of a wild cougar on the prowl. Of course there was the inevitable climax when the lion would discover his owner hiding in the brush. A joyful wrestling match would ensue between the two.

This game of hide and seek could work two ways. Birdie would disappear ahead of us. Although we knew what was going to happen, it would have been unfair to let on that we knew. So we would go down the trail, knowing full well that behind that boulder up ahead a cougar lurked. Sure enough, as soon as we had passed, Birdie would spring from behind the rock and land squarely on Ron's shoulder. There would be much hollering and growling. Soon the growling would turn to great throbbing purrs as the ferocious cat rolled over to be scratched. Fortunately these attacks were always directed toward Ron.

As filming progressed I could see that Birdie was beginning to accept me far more than I was ready to accept him. He was a beautiful cat and I told him so, and even scratched his belly. But I was a little unsure about the wrestling part of his friendship.

One afternoon we had set up a scene that would show Birdie standing atop a high projection of rock. He was supposed to be looking down toward a meadow below, but we hadn't been able to get him to look in the right direction. It was warm and the cougar needed some rest, so Ron let him lie down beneath a scrub oak. Then, while I went back up the slope and proceeded to reload my camera in the shade, Ron strolled down the cliff and out into the meadow.

Suddenly Birdie realized he was alone and raced to the edge of the cliff. Frantic, he began to look around for a way down. Then he spotted me a hundred yards away. There was an immediate change in his attitude; a look of relief was almost visible on his handsome face. With a devilish twitch of his tail he began loping toward me. I knew what was about to happen and frantically tried to get the camera back together, all the while shouting, "No, Birdie, no!" It did absolutely no good at all. With a leap he was on me. The camera was

Birdie Boy at about 3½ months.   (RICHARD T. BEEM)

He grew up with trust for humans.   (RICHARD T. BEEM)

knocked from my hands, and the film rolled down the hill. There was a moment of panic when I saw his huge jaws open. Then they closed gently on my shoulder; he was only playing. By the time Ron arrived, Birdie Boy's raspy tongue was swabbing my face and hair. He only wanted people, and for a moment he had thought we had deserted him.

After filming was finished, Birdie and Ron left. It was several years later that I learned of the cougar's fate. While Ron was away in the Army, Birdie was kept by an individual who wasn't too responsible at times. One night when the man was traveling through an Arizona town with the cat in his panel truck, he decided to pull over on a side street for some sleep. During the night Birdie somehow escaped from the van and made his way down dark streets. Eventually he entered the gate of a large manufacturing plant and was spotted by the night watchman. Naturally, the watchman was frightened. He

Ten months old and feeling his oats. (RICHARD T. BEEM)

fired a shot which missed the cat but sent him bounding away between darkened buildings.

The night watchman called the police, who arrived in force and began to comb the plant. For over an hour they searched while Birdie played his game of hide and seek. Only an occasional fleeting shadow betrayed the cat's presence. Finally he could wait no longer. It was time for the game to end. Brazenly he trotted around a corner toward the policemen, fully expecting to be greeted with kindness. Instead, a volley of shotgun and rifle blasts greeted him. He died not understanding their mistrust. And although it was a result of circumstances in which no one was to blame, it was a sad and unnecessary ending for Birdie Boy the friendly lion.

9

THE FLYING
SQUADRON

The cougar was the largest animal I ever worked with. From the largest I went to one of the smallest, the flying squirrel. An advertisement in an outdoors magazine suggesting flying squirrels as ideal pets caught my attention. Certainly here was a unique animal. It offered not only charm but an unusual physical adaptation which enables it to glide from tree to tree.

I clipped out the order form and sent a letter of inquiry to the "squirrel farm" in Texas. I received an immediate reply that they could supply me with one adult female and its two youngsters. Happily I sent payment and looked for the arrival of my new stars.

Several weeks later, when I had just about given up hope, a package arrived by air express. It was the strangest package the delivery man had ever seen. Apparently the Texan was not one for elaborate shipping cartons, because this was simply an old coffee can filled with paper excelsior and covered with wire screen. Considering the time it had taken for shipment, I wondered if the Texan had had to wait until he finished the can of coffee. The delivery man was extremely inquisitive about the contents of the "package." He was visibly disappointed when I signed for the package and chose not to open it in his presence.

Even after I had removed the screen and half the excelsior there still didn't appear to be anything in the package. Had I been taken? Then came a tiny rustling sound. Near the bottom, curled in a tight ball, were the mother squirrel and her two babies. The mother was no

Large eyes, long whiskers and a feathery tail make for a photogenic subject.   (AL SEYLE)

more than four inches long; her babies were half that length. I touched her and she looked up at me with huge, bulbous eyes and quivering whiskers. Her fur was soft gray and incredibly soft. In spite of the cramped conditions in the shipping container, she was perfectly groomed. From beneath their mother each baby, in turn, had a look at me. They were identical replicas of their parent, only smaller. Their eyes had a soft, trusting look that would have melted the hardest heart. Beside them were a few empty nut shells and a half-eaten orange from which they had gotten their nourishment while in transit. Their requirements were not great.

Although the mother was a bit wild, the babies soon tamed. Such delightful creatures! Fur as soft as down and a tail flat and light as a feather. They were soon climbing up and down my clothes, in and out of my shirt sleeves and collar. They were a little timid about jumping just yet but thoroughly enjoyed climbing about.

I kept the family in my den in a converted bird cage. By day they all slept in a tiny box filled with soft paper. Toward evening, however, they awoke and became active. A peanut shoved through the wire for each was almost a full meal. A water tube provided a source of water from which they drank frequently.

For the first two weeks the entire family stayed in the bird cage. Then, one evening, the youngsters discovered that they could get through the wire bars easily but their mother couldn't. This was, of course, most disturbing to Mom, for soon the babies were scurrying all around the room while she tried in vain to coax them home. These excursions usually lasted a half hour or more before they returned to the cage for a drink of water and a bit of peanut. Then they would be off again. They were extremely gentle and friendly animals. Every evening I familiarized myself with the little squirrels, and them with me, by handling them in play. They were the delight of visitors as they perched on a shoulder to eat a peanut. Their fur coats draped their bodies much like an oversized overcoat. Once they learned how to glide, however, it was clear that these extra folds of skin were used to form their flying surface. The door of my den was left closed during the night so that they could be free to roam. By morning the young ones would be snuggled safely back in the nest box with Mother.

One morning the youngsters were missing. I looked everywhere, under everything, and behind everything, in every conceivable hiding place. The door had been closed, so I was certain they couldn't have left the room. I was baffled. I double-checked every likely place, with no luck. Then I heard a stir above me. Hanging from my ceiling is a radio-controlled scale model of a World War I German fighter—the old open-cockpit type, with plenty of wires strung about—that I had built the year before and had hung there after having flown it three times and crashed it three times. Now, looking up, I saw two pairs of large eyes peering down at me from the cockpit of the Fokker. It was unbelievable. The tiny squirrels were in exact scale to the aircraft. With their goggle-like eyes they looked absolutely at home. I called the family, and everyone had a good laugh at the new pilots of the

Filming the flying squirrels requires a special enclosure to control them.

Fokker. It was a good place for them, I said. "After all, they're flying squirrels, you know."

A few weeks later I began to film them. Because flying squirrels are nocturnal, they were reluctant to work in full light at first. They had to be conditioned gradually, first in weak and then in brighter light. Finally they would eat and carry on most of their activity while I filmed. I gave them frequent breaks, however, to rest in the subdued light of their box. Since they were so small and so quick, special care was needed to capture them on film. They also were very difficult to catch, so I had to construct a special enclosure.

This enclosure couldn't be made of wire, which the squirrels would simply have climbed or gone through. A two-foot-high fence of solid, smooth plywood was effective. This circle of plywood could be set up around a stump or some other prop. It had to be far enough from the stump to prevent the animals from gliding over it. Once on the ground, the squirrels couldn't climb the smooth sides.

I used many different kinds of props within the enclosure to give a variety of scenes. Of course, the limitations of the enclosure prevented my getting any gliding scenes. I could get launching scenes off the stump, but no gliding.

The object of the film, of course, was to show off the unique gliding ability of flying squirrels. They do not truly fly, but glide on outstretched folds of skin. From the top of a tall tree they can often glide one hundred feet or more, landing like falling leaves on the forest floor.

It was obvious that I would have to change locations in order to film this aspect of the squirrels. I selected a large grassy area free of any trees, an area in which I could easily net the animals when they landed. I then constructed an elevated platform which would give them a high launching pad.

Since the rate of descent would be quite rapid, even though they were gliding, I chose to use a special camera which would film in superslow motion. Filming at a rate five times slower than normal, this camera would give five seconds of screen time for every second of actual time.

An assistant readied one of the squirrels atop the launching pad. The star was willing and eagerly surveyed the scene below. As the tiny animals always do before a launch, he bobbed up and down and sideways, measuring the trajectory—perhaps judging the distance by triangulation. Then he sprang from the platform and fluttered down in a gentle glide, to land on the soft grass. The entire drop had taken only two seconds, but on the screen it would be ten. Over and over we repeated the scene, until I was satisfied I could edit the footage properly.

The edited results were spectacular. The slow-motion camera revealed just how the loose skin folds between the front and hind legs catch the air like a parachute. The flat, feathery tail is used like an elevator on an aircraft to maintain the altitude of the glide. I was surprised to see that the little creatures can control their direction by dipping a foreleg in the direction they wish to go. The entire glide was a most graceful sight.

Filming proceeded without any problems, and the completed footage for the *Lassie* show received comments from people across the nation, because the public had seldom had the opportunity to see this shy animal in flight.

The squirrels stayed with us and lived for over four years, which is a long life for such tiny creatures.

Close-ups were easy with the friendly squirrels. (AL SEYLE)

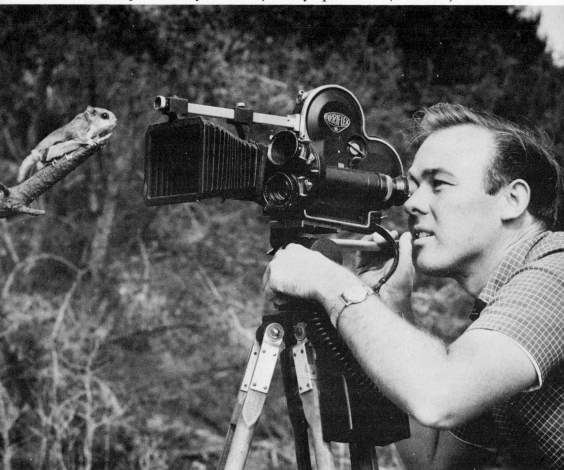

10

ISLAND FILMING

Above the roar of the aircraft engine I heard my father shout, as he pointed ahead and below us, "We're almost there, just below that fog bank." He closed the throttle of the Luscombe and glided toward the thin fog bank. In moments we were engulfed in white mist, and then we burst through into the clear.

Ahead, surrounded by the blue Pacific, lay a tiny dot of an island. Dad eased the throttle forward and leveled out as we approached the shore. I peered down to get a glimpse of the island of San Miguel, the westernmost of the Santa Barbara Channel Island group.

San Miguel is a lonely, windswept, uninhabited island situated fifty miles southwest of Santa Barbara, California. Like many people, I have always been intrigued by such islands. Their desolation and inaccessibility in a civilized world must appeal to the primitive element in us. Nearly everyone has, at one time or another, wished he could flee to his own private island.

The close proximity of the Santa Barbara Channel Islands to one of the most populated areas in the state makes them especially interesting. San Miguel, being the only uninhabited one, held particular interest for my father and me, and we had decided to make a film of it. With his skill as a bush pilot, we could have easy access to various portions of the island.

From the air we surveyed the land below. San Miguel is nine miles long, and three miles wide at its widest point. It is a low island, its highest point being only eight hundred feet above sea level. The

Our transportation to and from the island.

west end is sandy and windswept, while the east end is thickly covered
with grass. There is only one tree on the entire island.

Dad banked the plane sharply and dropped lower to examine a
possible landing site. As we swept low across a level stretch of sand
dunes, his eyes expertly scanned the terrain for potential hazards and
a good landing surface. Apparently satisfied, he cut a sharp turn,
dropped the flaps and glided in for a landing. I hoped he had calcu-
lated everything correctly. He had. We touched down as gently as a
falling leaf and rolled to a stop between two dunes, the extra-large
tires leaving a pair of wide tracks on the soft sand.

As we stepped out, I had an eerie feeling that we had somehow
landed on another planet. Around us was a weird setting, nothing of
which exists on the mainland. This northwest section of the island is
exposed to relentless winds which have carved the land deeply. Centuries ago a forest flourished in this area. A severe drought killed the

forest, and the subsequent drying of the land allowed the wind to cover the dead trees with sand. Over the intervening centuries the sand solidified around each branch and twig. As the present weather conditions arrived, the sand was slowly eroded away, to leave only casts of the ancient trees.

Walking among the remains of these trees, I was amazed at the perfect casts nature had created. Although the wood had long ago decomposed, it was easy to see the size and shapes of the trees. In some places only the tips of the trees were visible, but in others the wind had eroded the sand away until root structures were exposed. Being very brittle, the sand casts seldom protruded more than a foot or two above the sand surface.

In this strange landscape we began filming. The lunarlike landscape seemed appropriately absent of life. Harsh shadows and the absence of color added to the scene. Suddenly, almost imperceptibly, a pair of pointed ears rose above a nearby fossil trunk. The movement was ever so slight, yet it seemed grossly out of place. From behind another stump a hundred yards away another pair of ears emerged. Fifty yards to our right we got a fleeting glimpse of a gray shadow as it dashed from one stump to another. We were being watched. A tingle of excitement ran through me. I felt like an explorer setting foot for the first time on a strange planet and having his first contact with its inhabitants.

We pretended we didn't see the watchers and went about our business. Bit by bit the natives became bolder and exposed more of themselves. Now a small, pointed nose was visible as it tested the breeze to identify these alien visitors. It was an island fox, a subspecies of the mainland gray fox. We had heard that the island was inhabited by the little foxes and had looked forward to our first encounter.

As we worked, the shy animals followed us from place to place, keeping a discreet distance. But little by little they grew bolder and braver as their curiosity overcame their slight fear of man. It was a unique experience to have a "wild" fox follow us instead of bounding away in fright as it would have done on the mainland. On this isolated island the foxes have developed little fear of man, so infrequent are their encounters with humans.

Island gray fox, hoping for a handout.

We worked our way across the fossil forest until we came to the edge of the erosion. Ahead were several miles of thick grassland with frequent gullies and arroyos. This was the habitat of the fox. In the distance we could see several pairs of ears protruding from behind thick clumps of grass.

Dad set up the camera while I took up a position and attempted to coax one of the foxes to me. We had prepared for this by bringing a few tidbits of raw meat. I squeaked a sound, and the fox immediately perked up. Circling downwind, he tested the breeze and slowly came forward. I placed the piece of meat on the toe of my shoe and squeaked again. Now the fox was only ten feet away. I held still while he inched forward, leaned over, and daintily took the food from my shoe. Retreating a short distance, he gulped it down hastily. In this land of no rodents or reptiles, the foxes have a meager existence. Their diet consists mostly of insects and occasional birds. That one morsel of meat must have been a real banquet. Moments later he returned for seconds and thirds.

As we worked our way across this section of island we acquired a

122

following of several foxes. We felt like the Pied Pipers of San Miguel. Bit by bit we tossed our entire lunch to the hungry animals, and they accepted eagerly. The last thing to go was an apple. As it rolled down a hill, several foxes raced after it, biting chunks off and consuming them with relish. It was probably their first and last taste of fruit.

Since our landing spot was a difficult place for takeoffs, Dad decided he would take off alone and land on the west side, where I would meet him after hiking across the island. This was a frequent procedure as we filmed. Often he could land in a short space with the weight of two people and our equipment, but couldn't get off with the same weight. So, after filming in that area, I would hike to a better takeoff site. During that one summer we made twenty-five trips to San Miguel and I spent a good deal of time crisscrossing the island. These solitary walks were a very enjoyable part of the job.

San Miguel once supported a dense population of Indians. The remains of these prehistoric people and their tools are scattered profusely across the dunes. As I headed across this area I had only to look down to discover implements of various kinds. Mortars, pestles, whalebone tools for prying abalone from rocks, flat rocks for frying food, and countless other artifacts were scattered over several square miles. Mingled with them were the remains of the humans who had used them: a bleached leg bone protruding from a sand bank, the upper portions of a skull lying flat on the sand, its vacant eye sockets staring skyward. It was as if some giant grave robber had been hard at work searching for some ancient treasure. But it was not grave robbers, only the relentless wind which is forever uncovering graves and gently but firmly dislodging their contents. The graves uncovered today may be covered again tomorrow.

Near the center of the island were the remains of modern man's efforts to inhabit San Miguel. Nestled close to the hillside, in a vain attempt at protection from the ceaseless wind, was an old ranch house. It stood stalwart and weathered against the elements. Fifty years before it had housed a happy family and a few ranch hands who were determined to develop a sheep-raising business on the island. It was built from lumber salvaged from a wrecked schooner that had grounded on the treacherous west-end reef. The windward side of the U-shaped structure had only a few small portholes for light. That

West end of San Miguel Island—sea lions in the foreground, elephant seals in the background. (BILL BRISBY)

entire side of the building was covered with decades of moss and lichen growth and looked as if it had sprouted from the earth.

The old barn with its stables and corrals stood a hundred yards from the house. In the tack room the names of the horses were still vaguely visible above wooden pegs. Some of their equipment still hung, in tattered shreds, from the pegs. The only residents of the barn were a pair of ravens who scolded from the gable.

The sheep industry ended suddenly in San Miguel when the ranch manager took his own life. After burying him on a bluff overlooking Cuyler Harbor, his family returned to the mainland. Thus ended the last attempt to occupy San Miguel.

I headed west across the highest portion of the island. Looking down into a shallow valley, I saw the glint of metal. Upon closer investigation I discovered the twisted remains of a B-24 World War II bomber. On a training mission, it had plunged through dense fog with tremendous force into the center of the island. Thirteen men died in the crash. The incredible thing was that the wreckage had been undetected for thirteen years. Considering that it was clearly in the open, it is a good example of the loneliness of this island.

Climbing a last hill, I looked to the west, where in the distance was a beautiful white sandy beach. On the beach sat Dad's plane, and surrounding it were the bulky bodies of hundreds of elephant seals. I hurried onward, anxious to see these huge mammals.

On the bluff overlooking the shore stood a lonely shack built by the Navy for biologists to live in while studying the seals. Although the cabin was empty, I discovered that the door had been broken open. Upon investigation I saw a note scratched on the weathered door front: "Sorry to break in; have been stranded here ten days. Boat sank." Another mute testimonial to the loneliness of this island.

Down on the beach one could scarcely hear another voice, such was the din created by the herd of elephant seals. Hunted almost to extinction in the nineteenth century, the two-and-a-half-ton elephant seal has made a comeback along the California coast. This beach is one of the few breeding places for the giant mammals. The mass of brown bodies lying hide to hide for a quarter mile along the beach was a fantastic sight. As they lay, each seal would expertly flip sand with its flippers onto an insect-besieged portion of its body. Five hundred bodies flipping five hundred geysers of sand.

Frequent quarrels would break out between bull elephant seals. With loud roars, each participant would rear back and threaten the other, displaying his long, bulbous snout. It is this elephantlike nose of the males that gives the species its name. At the time we were on the island, in midsummer, these threat displays seldom came to blows. A few months earlier, however, the surf would be turned red as the bulls battled in the water for possession of the cows. Now it was only vestigial behavior from an earlier season.

Typical grouping of elephant seals. Mostly young bulls with their elephant noses. (BILL BRISBY)

On this same stretch of beach five other species of sea mammals breed, including the rare northern fur seal. San Miguel is the only place in the world where six species of sea mammals breed along the same sandy beach.

Our summer of filming revealed that San Miguel was the home of other rare forms of wildlife. A pair of bald eagles had a nest on a cliff overlooking a sheltered cove. Peregrine falcons also made daily appearances to pluck an easy meal from the vast colonies of shore birds.

At the time we were there, San Miguel was not protected from the vandalism of landing parties from pleasure craft. The discovery, on one trip, of dozens of dead newly born California sea lions made us realize that the wildlife there needed protection. Careless and ignorant people from a pleasure craft had frightened the herd into stampeding for the water, and the helpless young had been crushed beneath countless bodies. We left San Miguel feeling that something should be done to protect its unique environment.

Our film was shown throughout the United States on syndicated television and created enough interest to stimulate legislators to make it a part of the national park system. However, before it could come under the protection of government authority, fifteen years had passed; such are the ways of bureaucratic red tape. In the interim the island was plundered and its wildlife harassed. Bald eagles and peregrine falcons left. The breeding colonies of sea lions were greatly disturbed by the curious. Even the once tame island foxes had learned to fear man, for landing parties used them for target practice. The climax came when a Navy aircraft accidentally fired a missile at the island, setting it afire. The entire grassy portion was burned and much damage was done to the environment. It was a fiery climax to the controversy over the future of the island. The Navy, which wanted San Miguel for a bombing target, very nearly had its way. Today this small spot of land has a temporary reprieve as part of the Channel Island National Park system. With proper protection and care, San Miguel may survive and regain its unique wildlife habitat.

Older bull keeps a watchful eye on the camera.   (BILL BRISBY)

The coastal waters along this part of California are a rich marine environment. I have had occasion to film many varieties of its wildlife. From the white sands of San Miguel I traveled, years later, to Anacapa, the eastern island in the chain, on whose rugged cliffs is one of the few remaining breeding colonies of brown pelicans in California.

Through special permission of park and wildlife authorities, I was now approaching the sheer cliffs of Anacapa's north side. My helicopter pilot expertly selected a flat spot and set us down gently. After unloading my gear I reminded the pilot to return in two days, and watched as he throbbed his way back across the channel.

I was met a few minutes later by a young research biologist who had been studying the plight of the pelicans for several months. He led me to the edge of the cliff, where the nesting colony was visible several hundred yards away. He informed me that there were almost five hundred nests on the island and as yet there had not been one successful hatching.

This was the dilemma which now faced the species. Due apparently to the toxic level of pesticides in the parents, the eggs of the brown pelican were not hatching. The development of the eggshell was retarded, producing eggs with shells too thin to withstand incubation. The biologist showed me several flattened eggs he had collected from nests. It was, he said, a disastrous year for the pelicans.

I readied my camera and began to film nesting behavior. As I filmed I was struck by the irony of what I saw in the viewfinder. A male pelican was going through his courtship ritual of showing his red gular pouch and delivering twigs to his mate. Moments later they both sailed out over the water and plunged with identical precision to catch a fish. That very fish was, no doubt, contaminated with pesticides which began as spray on crops miles distant and was ultimately washed into the sea. The pelicans' meal of that fish, and others, would give them the energy to complete nest building, but would also contribute to the deformity of the very egg for which they were preparing.

For two days I filmed the nesting activity of the Anacapa colony of pelicans. When I left I felt sad at the collision which was occurring between, on the one hand, man and his technology and, on the other, the wildlife and its needs. Time will tell the story of the pelicans. As for that year, only one baby pelican was produced by the nests of over five hundred pairs. A pathetic side effect of man's march of progress.

Although progress threatens some species, at times it helps others by eliminating the need for the commercial exploitation of the species. One such species is the largest fish found in these waters, the basking shark. Until recently this thirty-foot monster was hunted for its valuable oil, hide and vitamins. But new developments in chemistry have produced synthetic substitutes so that it is no longer necessary to hunt the fish.

My first filming experience with the sharks was from a small boat. We were eight miles from shore on a perfectly calm day and were absolutely thrilled with the prospects for filming. My father previously had spotted a huge school of basking sharks from his airplane, and now we were attempting to get in close by boat.

Although I had seen the monstrous fish before when the shark boats brought them into the harbor, I wasn't prepared to see them moving freely about in the water. Our first glimpse was a bit frightening to me. Ahead of us there suddenly appeared dozens of huge dorsal fins on the glassy surface. These fins were hard to ignore, because they protruded above the water a full three feet. The shocking thing was that the tail fin cut the surface more than twenty feet behind the dorsal fin! Our frail boat was only sixteen feet in length.

In moments we were in the midst of the school. We cut the engine and drifted. True to their name, the sharks were basking in the sun, right on the surface. Frequently one of the monsters would glide by our boat with mouth wide open as it strained the water for plankton. Often we could look directly down the huge mouth and throat. We were getting marvelous footage of the sharks as they swam unconcernedly around us. I had to remind myself constantly that they were not man-eaters. Basking sharks eat only microscopic plankton and are in fact quite harmless to man.

The dozens of fins breaking the surface around us looked like so many tombstones in a graveyard. In view of the somber and dangerous appearance of the scene, my father decided to inject a bit of humor into the film. His brilliant idea was to have me rope one of the dorsal fins. Somewhat reluctantly I agreed to give it a try. I headed the boat toward the biggest shark we could find. While Dad filmed I eased up alongside the fish, threw a rope around the fin, and gave it a good tug just for the camera's sake.

There was an instant reaction on the part of the shark. One wouldn't think a creature that size would be so sensitive about one tiny part of its anatomy. Not overjoyed with the idea of having its dorsal fin fooled with, it burst into life with a powerful sweep of its tail. Like the tail of a horse swishing away an annoying fly, the shark's tail caught us squarely. Boat and its occupants were sent skidding sideways across the water. Thank goodness the fish didn't hold grudges. It submerged and never reappeared. But we did have some fine footage of a fool trying to rope a thirty-foot shark from a boat half that size.

It was many years later when I again had contact with a basking shark. This time I was assisting a cameraman as he filmed a sequence for the feature picture *Ring of Bright Water*, the story of a Scotsman and his two pet otters. Director-photographer Jack Couffer had made arrangements to buy a shark carcass for the scene, from one of the few remaining shark fishing boats. (The carcasses of the sharks by this time were being used only to make fertilizer.)

It was a bizarre scene, one in which the make-believe of movie making and the reality of life were intertwined. In the film, the shark carcass was to be a source of food for the two otters. It was not improbable that their owner would turn to such an easy source of food as one huge shark; it would feed the otters for a long time. Our job was to get on film the sequence which showed the man and a girl laboriously chopping up the carcass on the beach and hauling it, bucket by bucket, up the shore to a giant freezer. It was here that make-believe and reality were one and the same.

Since the fish weighed well over three tons, it was a gigantic undertaking. The director wanted the final scene to show the entire fish defleshed, like the remains of a trout on a plate. That meant hauling away more than two tons of flesh, bucket by bucket.

The boat crew members carved most of the flesh away without

camera. Then, with camera, the two actors got into position while the rest of us looked on. The male actor carved a huge chunk and dropped it into a bucket held by the girl. Then the girl turned dutifully and hauled the load up the shore.

Over and over the scenes were done, with the girl always hauling. The fish got smaller with excrutiating slowness. The sheer magnitude of the task necessitated a lot of time and work. The actors were supposed to portray fatigue, but they didn't need to act. It was very natural.

After an hour or two a small group of people gathered on the beach to watch. None of them knew what was going on, but all were keenly interested in the shark. Never had they seen such a monster. So engrossed were they in the fish that most didn't even notice the camera.

One old gentleman surveyed the situation with growing disgust. By now the shark was almost completely cut up and the actress was staggering under each load that her otter-obsessed companion gave her. The film was to depict the utter absurdity of it all as the girl struggled to please her friend.

Finally the old gentleman onlooker could stand it no more. He was completely unaware of the camera. The only thing he saw was a slip of a girl struggling to carry the heavy buckets while at least a dozen strong men looked on without even offering to help. He might not be much, but, by Jove, he sure could help some! With classic Victorian gallantry he strode boldly before the camera and said in a clear, unmistakably disgusted voice, "Here, young lady, let me help you with that."

The scene had to be retaken, of course, but it was obvious that the message had come across very clearly.

11

LIFE IN
DEATH VALLEY

The road ahead was long and straight, and it dropped in a gentle descent toward the distant white valley. I put my van into neutral and coasted mile after mile, enjoying the free ride and the stark landscape about me.

Rocky soil with scattered creosote bushes stretched to distant hills with barren, lifeless contours. I couldn't help marveling at the ease with which modern man crosses this desert. The early pioneers struggled with great difficulty to cross by the very route I was now speeding along.

Lower and lower the road dropped; now I was below sea level. I was entering Death Valley, a place noted for its severe weather conditions and harsh environment. In this so-called wasteland I was to produce a documentary on endemic wildlife.

I had researched my subject well before beginning the film. From my investigation I became convinced that Death Valley was one of the most misunderstood places in the United States. It had perhaps had more tall tales told about it than any other area in the country. Over the years the bleakness of the landscape had become legendary. Is was, most people thought, a wasteland without life.

The very name Death Valley stirs up visions of beleaguered bands of pioneers struggling in vain to cross the arid flatlands, dropping one by one by the wayside. And it's true that a band of Forty-Niners, the Bennett-Arcane party, suffered extreme hardships crossing the valley. But as to the outcome of that three-week ordeal there are conflicting stories. Some people say that all the members of the party died in the valley. Others say that only one survived to tell the story. The truth is that all but one person survived. As they were led across the Pana-mint Mountains, they paused to look back on the valley they had thought would be the grave of them all, and someone muttered, "Goodbye, Death Valley." And Death Valley had its name.

In the last half of the last century, activity flourished in the mountains around the valley. Silver and gold ore were discovered, and the rush was on. Booming mining camps and towns sprang up overnight, legends were established daily. Landmarks, canyons and mountain ranges were named by the mining people. Today the mines are empty and the towns are dead, but the names live on.

These descriptive names are probably partially responsible for today's popular concept of Death Valley. As the valley is approached from the east, the traveler passes through the Last Chance range of mountains. If he survives that, he will enter the Funeral Range. He may pass Coffin Canyon or Arsenic Springs. The best view of the

Death Valley from the Panamints.

valley is from Dante's View; from there the visitor may see the Devil's Golf Course or the Devil's Hay Field. There are other features, such as Furnace Creek, Badwater, Salt Creek, and the Devil's Racetrack, which all indicate that here is a land that is less than habitable. It is normal, therefore, for people to assume that there is little wildlife here. It was this misconception that I would attempt to clear up in my film.

Biologists have studied the valley closely and have accurately indexed its wildlife. There is an amazing abundance of life secreted within its dry walls. Over six hundred species of plants, including ten ferns, six lilies and two wild orchids, are on the botanical list. The list of fauna found in the valley includes over three hundred species of birds and fifty species of mammals.

The challenge facing me was to get good footage of a cross section of this plant and animal life and weave it into an entertaining and informative film. My decision to do the film had been met with some skepticism on the part of friends and relatives because they too were influenced by the traditional layman's view of Death Valley. I must admit that I wondered to myself, as I rolled into the valley, if I would find sufficient material.

At National Park Service headquarters I introduced myself to Dwight Warren, chief naturalist, and told him of my intentions. He was very cooperative and immediately began to map out areas where I might see certain kinds of wildlife. One of the first things I should film, he said with a twinkle in his eye, was the flamingo that had just arrived at a nearby pond. Half expecting some kind of joke, I followed his directions to the pond. Sure enough, there was a real live flamingo wading contentedly in the water. The sight of the tropical bird against the background of such stark desert was astounding.

I immediately set up my camera and began filming. I was lucky enough to get several takeoffs with the flamingo circling gracefully out over the valley. Where the flamingo had come from I don't know. Escaped from a zoo, most likely, since flamingos are not found naturally within the United States. But even the nearest zoo was over three hundred miles away. In order to find this tiny spot of water, the flamingo must have had to cross hundreds of miles of desert and climb thousands of feet over mountains. It was an incredible introduction to Death Valley and pointed out dramatically that in nature the un-expected is always just around the corner.

There are many such corners in Death Valley, as I soon found. Winding my way down Titus Canyon one afternoon, I was struck by the sight of the polished vertical walls that rose two hundred feet above me. The canyon was so narrow that my vehicle could barely slip through. Often, during rainstorms, rushing flash-flood waters fill these canyons, but now Titus was only a dry, dusty, boulder-strewn crack in the mountains.

Rounding a bend, I suddenly came upon a spot of green at the base of a bare cliff, and a small pool of water no larger than a bathtub. Growing in profusion at the very edge of the pool were hundreds of wild orchids—delicate, tiny flowers, so out of place in this canyon as to make one suspect that a practical joker stood just around the next bend, laughing at his latest creation. I bent down and examined the flowers and began to photograph their delicate violet-streaked

Kangaroo rat. He never drinks water.

throats. Suddenly a buzz of wings startled me as a tiny Costa's hummingbird, its purple gorgets flashing in the sun, arrived to partake of the drop of nectar that awaited him at each flower. For several minutes I was lost in a world of orchids and hummingbirds as I filmed. Then the harsh call of a raven awakened me to my desert environment. I hurried on down the dry canyon, marveling at the tiny oasis I had found.

If the orchids were atypical of this valley, then the kangaroo rat was the most typical. This tiny rodent lives in profusion across the valley floor, and evidence of his presence can be found in the numerous holes that dot the ground. He is marvelously adapted for desert life, since he never has to drink water in his entire life. His body manufactures water through the oxidation of carbohydrates in the dry seeds he eats.

My first experience with this delightful animal came one night by my campfire. From the edge of darkness a small cream-colored body bounced toward the fire. I sat immobile as the bannertail bounced like a Ping-Pong ball up to my feet. There he began to nibble on some bread crumbs I had dropped. Slowly I moved, and he seemed not in the least alarmed. I extended another piece of bread and he accepted. Because of his friendly ways, this animal is perhaps the most delightful of desert creatures. I caught him with my hat and gently held him in my hands. His cream-colored fur was as soft as silk. The kangaroo rat's extremely long tail, which is used as a balancing pole as he hops kangaroo style, is covered with fur and has a silky tassel at the tip. Long, sensitive whiskers and round, bulbous eyes equip the animal for nocturnal life.

I relaxed my hold and released him in my lap. Instead of leaping away, he turned and began to explore my shirt. In minutes he was inside the shirt, busy investigating this new habitat. Gently I extracted him and dropped him to the ground. After leisurely exploring the camp area, he retreated into the blackness.

A few days later I began to film a sequence in the magnificent sand dunes at the center of the valley. As I walked the quiet dunes, composing scenes of the delicate wind-etched patterns, I noticed everywhere the telltale tracks of kangaroo rats—two hind-feet prints and a tail mark as they bounced bipedal across the sand. This was the

Rat and sidewinder confront each other.

Rat at home in burrow built by Kent.

place, I decided, to film a sequence of this animal's behavior. That night I trapped a beautiful specimen by the light of my fire.

I had no lighting system, so I was forced to film by daylight even though this was not the natural activity period for the rat. In order to make it appear more natural on film, I filmed it "day for night," a technique by which daylight is made to appear as moonlight on the screen. In this way, I felt, the audience would more readily accept the rat's activity.

His first reaction upon being exposed to daylight was to seek a burrow. I had expected this and had carefully selected the spot, making sure there were no holes nearby. I got good footage of the rat bouncing back and forth across the dunes. Finally he began to dig a new hole at the base of a creosote bush. This produced fine film of the little fellow at work.

Moments later the unexpected happened. From beneath a nearby creosote bush an ominous buzzing began. Although it was midday and in the month of January, when such creatures should be hibernating, a sidewinder rattlesnake emerged. I was delighted that he should appear at this opportune moment. I still don't know why he appeared on such a cool winter day, but I lost no time in getting my camera ready.

In filming animals it is important to know their behavior. There are certain reactions that one can expect from animals in response to certain stimuli. If the photographer is observant and quick, these reactions can be recorded on film. If he is not aware of the impending reactions, he is likely to be caught unawares and miss the shot.

The instant I saw the snake I knew what kind of footage I could get. From previous knowledge I knew that the snake would seek a dark place, and at the moment he was heading directly for the creosote bush under which the rat was digging. I also knew what reaction the rat would have upon seeing the sidewinder, its archenemy.

In its peculiar sideways fashion, the slender reptile moved toward the bush. From the sides of its flat, horned head slit-pupil eyes were fixed on the shadows of the bush. Frequently its forked tongue flicked out and there was a spasmodic buzz of rattles. The snake was agitated, having been disturbed by my movements around his daytime retreat.

Under the bush the rat was busily working on his hole, which was now about six inches deep. At periodic intervals, he would emerge to shove sand away from the entrance. It was during one of the rat's earth-moving operations that the snake arrived on the scene. To the snake, the burrow was the logical place to head for protection from the sun.

The instant the rat saw the snake, not more than three inches in front of him, he sprang straight up a foot or more and landed a foot back. Then he began to behave exactly as I suspected he would. It is an age-old, inherent behavior pattern built into the animal. With his strong hind feet he kicked sand directly into the face of the sidewinder. The results were predictable. The snake flinched and retreated in the face of this mini-sandstorm. This gave the rat the necessary time to escape the threat of the snake.

Although this sequence occurred in daylight, it was typical of the reaction of the rat whenever confronted with its enemy. No doubt this behavior is repeated countless times every night as predator and prey seek to survive. By knowing in advance the behavior pattern, I was able to capture it on film.

From one end of Death Valley to the other I traveled, filming the incongruities of this fascinating place. At the far northern portion on a dry lake bed is a mystery which still puzzles and confuses scientists. There on the flat lake bed lie many large boulders weighing several hundred pounds each. Behind each a trail is gouged in the mud, as if a giant unseen hand had reached down from the sky and dragged the boulder along. Scientists aren't sure how they moved. The most believable explanation is that strong winds inched the boulders along when the lake bed was slick with winter rain.

At the extreme southern end of the valley I visited a delightful and very remote place called Saratoga Springs. Here is truly a natural desert oasis, where fresh water flows year round from the base of a rust-red mountain. Several acres of ponds and marshes provide a wonderful habitat for visiting waterfowl as well as land birds. Geese, egrets, herons, and countless songbirds use its quiet water and sedges.

Near the base of the red mountain in a deep crystal pool subterranean water bubbles constantly. Here in this pool is yet another kind of life in the midst of the harsh desert. Thousands of tiny fish called desert pupfish live here and in adjacent ponds. A last remnant of an age when the entire valley was a vast inland lake, these fish now live their aquatic life in the center of one of the world's driest deserts.

Much of my filming was done around the various water holes and mesquite thickets. One of my favorite water holes was a pond near Furnace Creek Ranch, a tourist center (Death Valley, a national monument, is visited by over five hundred thousand people annually), and I often encountered bird watchers and other nature enthusiasts there.

Probably the strangest experience in my filming career came one afternoon as I approached this pond. I usually made the rounds of

Chuckwalla lizard, a harmless vegetarian.

Desert bighorn sheep, a dwindling species.

my favorite filming spots every couple of days to see what new varieties of ducks and other birds had arrived. On my previous visit to this place I had filmed an excellent sequence of a coyote stalking some shoveler ducks at the edge of the pond. Now, hoping for another rare shot, I crept up on the location cautiously, with camera ready. But in spite of my caution I inadvertently stepped on a dry twig. Immediately in the thicket ahead of me there was the sound of something running. It sounded large, and my heart pounded as I raced to a clearing. Probably a bighorn sheep, I thought. I hastily plopped down my tripod and pointed the camera toward the noise.

An instant later a figure burst into the clearing and raced at full gallop toward another thicket. My hasty camera adjustments were stopped short when I saw that my subject was a man, stark naked! With utter abandon he plunged headlong into another thorny mesquite thicket and disappeared. And then I realized that I had broken a cardinal rule of photography: Regardless of what happens, don't stop filming! I had missed the shot of the year as far as Death Valley wildlife goes.

In filming wildlife in its natural habitat, much time and patience is required. The photographer's success is dictated largely by pure luck—being in the right place at just the right moment—so there is usually much wasted time. At Death Valley I spent countless hours and even days waiting patiently for something exciting to happen.

Selecting a site for the setting up of a camera blind calls for much forethought. Usually I would set up near some natural attraction for wildlife, such as a water hole, a nest or a favorite perch for birds. Often these locations were chosen as a result of observations I had made of an animal or bird's behavior from a distance. For instance, if I observed a coyote pass by a certain spot nearly every evening at a certain time, or a red-tailed hawk return habitually to a particular tree perch, there would be a good chance that if I were set up at that location I could get a good shot.

In the Panamint Mountains on Death Valley's west side I observed one day, from the road, a pair of golden eagles a mile away, soaring around a high bluff. Several times thereafter I saw the same pair soaring gracefully about the cliff. I soon realized that this was one of their favorite soaring sites, since the prevailing wind created good lift on the slope.

It was, by all indications, a good place to build a blind. From the top of the cliff I could get a spectacular scene if the eagles arrived, as they seemed to, every day. The next day I laboriously carried my blind to the top of the cliff. It was difficult work, since the terrain was very rough, and I stopped frequently to rest in the shade of large rock formations.

On one of these rest stops I heard suddenly, from high above me, an increasing roar of wind, climaxing in a loud swoosh. A golden eagle plunged past me and pulled up steeply in a graceful maneuver. It was a breathtaking sight as the great bird soared on outstretched wings above the distant valley. Moments later the eagle veered off and disappeared around a bend.

Eagerly I finished the climb and set up my blind. I camouflaged it as best I could and returned down the mountainside. It would take the eagles a few days to accept the blind; I would work elsewhere in the meantime.

Two weeks later I arrived at the location. From the road below I scanned the mountains with my binoculars. My blind was still in position. For several hours I watched from my car. In the late afternoon when the breeze came up the two eagles arrived at the site. Gracefully they soared back and forth, directly in front of my blind. I was elated and could vividly visualize the wonderful shots I would get the next day. I drove my camper off the main road a short distance and prepared for the night.

Before dawn I began the long climb up the cliff. In the blackness the hill contour looked unfamiliar and I groped awkwardly for footholds among the rocks. I was thankful for the cold because no rattlesnake would be out. After an hour I found my blind and entered. I burned short twigs in a tiny fire to keep my hands warm and passed the time until dawn.

With the arrival of day, the panorama below unfolded in a soft glow of gold and purple hues. The silence was pure and untarnished. Only the early-morning calls of the ravens and the distant brays of wild burros floated on the still air. I knew that somewhere on the cliffs nearby the two eagles were preparing to meet the new day. Probably even now they were preening and grooming their feathers for the day's activities. I leaned back against a rock and, with great satisfaction, watched the sun's first rays play over the desert.

As the morning progressed, a variety of birds took advantage of the ideal slope for soaring. Red-tailed hawks and ravens arrived and departed with regularity. Tiny white-throated swifts darted back and forth with seemingly perpetual motion as they pursued their insect prey. About midday a prairie falcon with slender pointed wings arrived to soar the slope. I watched as this speedy predator arced across the cobalt sky and then stooped with incredible speed to snatch a meadowlark from the valley below.

From time to time cars passed along the highway a mile to the west. Around midafternoon a green pickup stopped at the roadside, and a man began to look intently at my camper parked a half mile off the road. Through my binoculars I could see that it was a park ranger and that he was very interested in the presence of my camper in an unauthorized area. Although I had cleared my setup with park headquarters, the ranger below probably knew nothing of my authorization. He began to walk toward my camper.

From my elevated position I had an excellent view of the ranger's activity. Obviously he suspected that the camper's occupants were up to no good, because he began to stalk the vehicle as if it housed a gang of desperados. Down a gully he crept, rising up from time to time to orient himself. From the gully he made a crouched mad dash for a large boulder. There he scrutinized the camper closely through binoculars. For several minutes he pondered the situation. I figured he was weighing his chances: should he try to capture the gang single-handedly or should he go for reinforcements? He looked again through his binoculars. Still no sign of life. Probably a trap.

Once again he crouched low and crept along a dry wash. He was distracted momentarily by a shiny object in the brush. He picked up the discarded soup can (not mine) and examined it thoroughly, as if it might be a clue to the identity of the gang. The presence of only one soup can seemed to reassure him, for now he boldly walked up and peered into the camper. After checking the vehicle thoroughly and jotting down the license number, he began a detailed observation of the mountainside on which I was hidden.

It was extremely interesting to watch his progress as he studied the hillside. I knew he would see the blind sooner or later. There was a visible reaction when he spotted the burlap structure hidden between two boulders. I could almost feel the satisfaction he must have had at that moment. After looking for several minutes, he jumped to his feet and almost ran back to his truck.

From the cab he extracted a tripod and mounted on it a powerful telescope. Through his binoculars he had seen the blind, but he

wanted a real close look. By now I had ceased to watch through my binoculars and was observing through the 300-millimeter lens of my camera because it had twice the power.

I watched as the ranger adjusted his scope and zeroed in on the hillside. There were a few moments as he searched for my blind through his scope, and then he had me. From his point of view all he could see was a sheet of burlap and, in the center, the black barrel of my lens peering right back at him.

For a moment he looked intently and then the whole thing began to soak in. Someone was behind the eye in the blind, watching him, and obviously had been watching ever since he arrived. Suddenly he felt foolish and grossly exposed. Trying to appear casual, he sheepishly put away his equipment and, without another glance in my direction, sped away.

I stayed in the blind for the next two days, but never once saw the two eagles. A few days later, however, while I was leaving the area, two eagles chased a rabbit back and forth across the road before my car. Finally one of them caught the animal no more than a hundred yards from me. With my camera mounted in the camper I was able to film a sequence of the eagles right through the open door at very close range. It was an incredible climax, after all my hours of waiting atop that mountain, to get such a sequence from the door of my car.

The afternoon was still and the soft hum of countless insects seemed to accentuate the stillness. I sat immobile atop a high sand dune and absorbed the solitude. Around me the dunes stretched their soft contours in every direction. Delicate patterns etched on the surface were enhanced by the late sun.

It was late spring and the days would soon be blistering with traditional Death Valley heat. Most of the tourists were gone and I was ending the second season of filming in this land. I watched as an Eleodes beetle plodded its way up a dune, leaving behind a delicate crocheted trail. He crested the dune and hurried down the steep slope, unmindful of the vast distance he must go before finding vegetation.

In the distance a Gambel's quail called, and closer I heard the

OPPOSITE: *Sand dune artistry.*

coo-coo call of a roadrunner. I knew that with nightfall, coyotes, foxes, and owls would take up their parts in the desert chorus.

My filming was ending, I had only a few last shots, and would return home to begin editing. Reluctantly I thought about leaving this valley. Over the months of plodding its floor and canyons I had

Roadrunner, desert speedster.

become acquainted with a friendly land. I watched a car speed along the distant highway. A last visitor, no doubt, anxious to see the valley in a single day. Of the half million people who have been here in the last year, only a few have really seen the valley, I thought. Those who took the time to really look were immensely rewarded.

I remember the small stream at the base of Grapevine Mountains, choked with watercress and alive with frogs. Or, at the opposite end of the scale, the kangaroo rat with his self-contained water-manufacturing ability. The creosote bush which emits a poison from its roots to kill other plants so it won't have competition for water. The sight of Panamint daisies bursting into full bloom from amid dry rocks, or the orchids in dry Titus Canyon. The incongruity of a flamingo in the valley, or desert pupfish at Saratoga Springs.

It is a land that presents a harsh veneer to the casual visitor. It is not a land where beauty in traditional forms shouts out at the on-looker. Rather, it is a beauty that lies beneath the dry, prickly shrubs and rocky soil. It requires that one scratch below the surface. I hoped that my film would do just that.

A year later I began a lecture tour for the National Audubon Society, showing my film "Death Valley, Land of Contrast." Before one of my first shows I overheard a woman speak to her companion. "I've always wanted to go to Death Valley, Ethel, but I'm just terrified of the place." I knew that thousands of other Americans felt that way, too.

One evening before a show I was talking to two small boys who were full of questions about Death Valley. One looked at me seriously and asked, "Do they got a lot of skulls out there?" I asked the other boy what he knew about Death Valley. He thought quietly for a moment and then said, "Well, one thing I have heard. They say that once you go there you never come back!" And then he brightened and said, "But you came back!" I could see that my film would not be wasted on this audience, and probably not on any other, for that matter.

12

REFLECTIONS
FROM THE FOREST

The twelve-thousand-foot elevation and the forty pounds of camera equipment were having their effect on me. After having hiked up the steep slope of loose dolomite soil, I was puffing like a steam engine. I sat down on a white ledge to rest. In the late-afternoon light the trees around me had a new dimension. Here in the White Mountains of California stood the oldest living things on this earth, the ancient bristlecone pine trees. Their weathered trunks took on a golden glow which seemed to accentuate the fact that these trees had survived thousands of years of severe weather conditions.

As the pounding of my heart subsided, I was conscious of the extreme quiet around me. For several days I had been filming in this forest, and its very solitude seemed to add a note of reverence to the scene. Before me stood the twisted and contorted shape of a four-thousand-year-old tree. Its branches and trunk revealed a tortured existence which had endured severe winds, drought, ice storms and heavy snow. I waited in the dimming light for just the right moment when the sunset colors would provide the perfect background for this ancient sculpture.

A silent shadow winged across the slope below and swooped up to land on a gnarled tree. The great horned owl assumed a posture with ear tufts erect and became immobile, a part of the tree itself, it seemed. I smiled, remembering my first experience with horned owls many years before. Since that long-ago introduction, I have

Thousands of years have sculpted these ancient bristlecone pines.

had many experiences with these nocturnal birds. So much so that it seemed I knew that owl on the bristlecone personally.

In the gathering twilight, my mind was drawn back to the question of how my work had benefited me. More than anything else, I was happy doing it. And there had grown an awareness of things about me that was invaluable. In reflecting, I realized how much I treasured my experiences with creatures I had had the privilege to know through film making—from the comical antics of raccoons, otters and prairie dogs to the serious behavior of sandhill cranes in courtship or bull elk rutting for dominance.

I have had the opportunity to film many species of wildlife that are struggling for survival in today's world, and am concerned now, more than ever, about their fate.

In Florida, that vast, watery flatland that supports an abundance of wildlife, I filmed the nesting of the wood ibis in Corkscrew Swamp. It was the first year in three that the storks had nested. So critical is their need for proper water level in their feeding areas that if it is not correct they will not nest. Man's tampering with the water of the Everglades has altered the natural water level.

Not far away I filmed the rare Everglade kite, a bird which subsists on a large species of snail. Since the snail is its sole source of food, even the most ignorant person could understand how a lack of snails could affect the kite. The same water problem that affects the storks has also caused a serious decline in the snails and, consequently, a slow decline in the graceful Everglade kite.

Closer to home, along the Southern California coast, the change has been subtle but as relentless as a glacier movement. In the twenty-five years since I scrambled over the boat decks to gather sardines, this abundant fish has entirely vanished from the Pacific Coast. Not a single sardine has been caught commercially for fifteen years.

The bald eagles and peregrine falcons which greeted us when my father and I first visited San Miguel Island are no longer found in this part of California. Even the brown pelicans, which are as much a part of the coast as the surf itself, are slowly succumbing to the pressures of man's progress.

Not only the wildlife is suffering, but the land as well. More than once I have accidentally captured on film a piece of paper hanging on a distant bush or the glint of the sun from a discarded beverage bottle or can. Filming in the desert is getting difficult because of the many off-road vehicle tracks that crisscross the ground. In a forest it is often carved initials on a tree trunk that disturb an otherwise perfect scene.

The very survival of all creatures, including man, depends upon their sensitivity to their environment. For some it is only a primitive sensitivity to light and dark, dry and moist, heat and cold. For others it is a delicate, advanced sensitivity to sounds, odors, sights or weather conditions which enables them to understand their surroundings. The human observer, therefore, must develop his senses in order to be in

American egret.

Wood stork approaching nest with a twig in its bill.

Nesting colony of wood storks in the Everglades.

tune with nature. This sensitivity is a vital side effect of a closeness with nature, because it can be used in relations with fellow man.

From down in the canyon I heard the unmistakable attempt of a young horned owl trying to hoot. The adult on a bristlecone answered with throaty professionalism. The sky was now rich in color, and the ancient bristlecone before me cut a crisp, sculptured pattern against it.

I framed the scene properly in the view finder and rolled the film. It was to be a long scene, one in which music would be combined with the pictorial beauty as a climax to the film on the ancient

Patience and plenty of time, two elements necessary for a wildlife photographer.

Jackson Hole, Wyoming, a wildlife paradise.

California ground squirrel.

Wyoming ground squirrel scolds the photographer.

forest. In the midst of the take a Clark's nutcracker landed on an uppermost branch, adding a final, perfect touch to a lovely scene. I finished the take and resumed my place on the rock. I was the lone spectator to the extravaganza spread before me.

The sky was now deep purple and the first stars twinkled an evening greeting. A faint glow to the east gave promise of a full moon. In the near darkness I shouldered my camera and began the trek down the mountainside. In the silence my noisy footsteps seemed an unnecessary intrusion. I felt enriched from the experience of the past few hours. It was but a few moments of a lifetime, but moments I would not have traded for anything. I thought of Thomas Carlyle's statement, "The tragedy of life is not so much what men suffer, but rather what they miss." I was glad I had not missed this experience.

Beaver, in Utah.

End of a day's filming at an Everglades pond.